JN297609

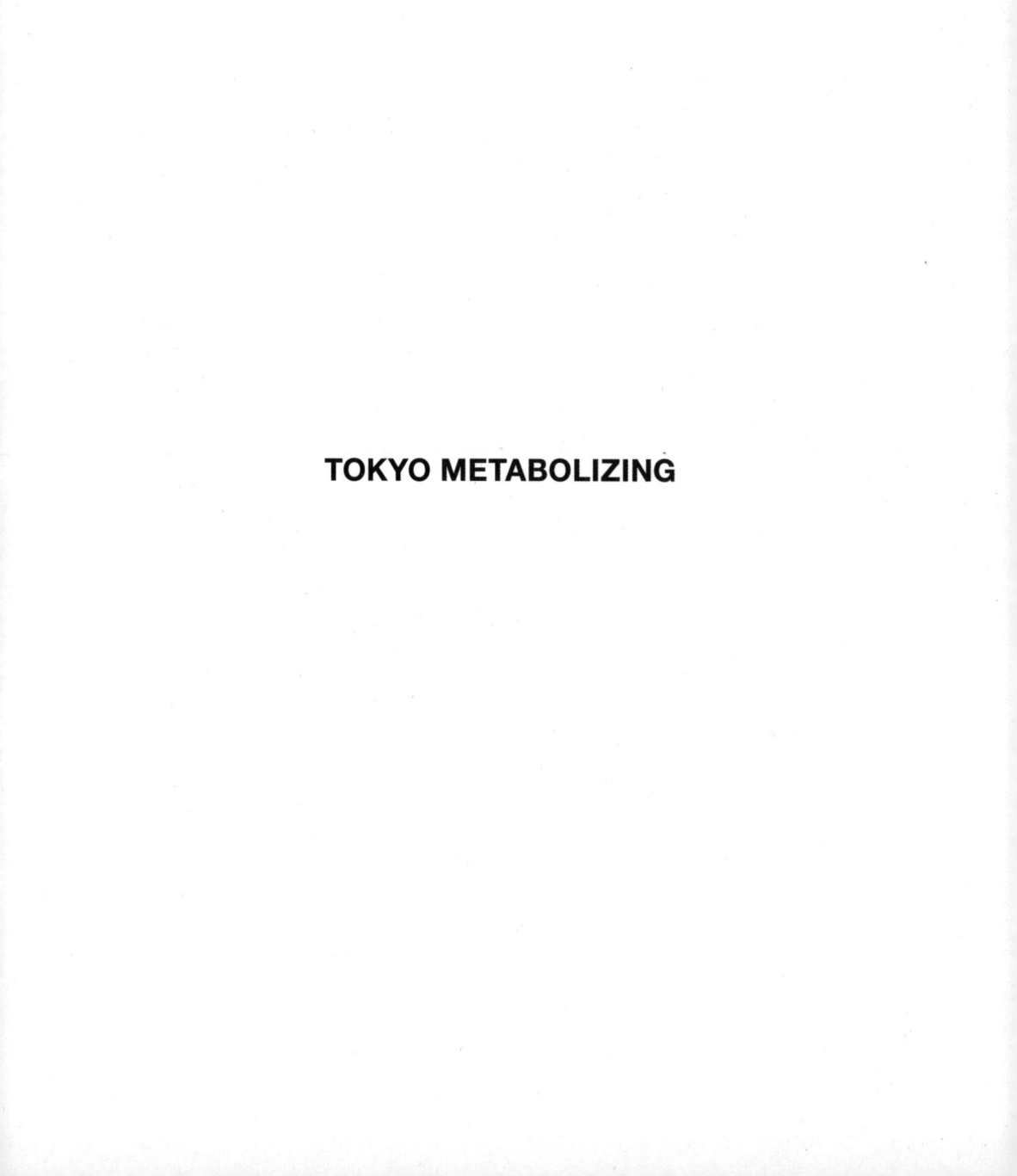

TOKYO METABOLIZING

TOKYO METABOLIZING

First published in Japan on July 25, 2010
Fifth published on September 30, 2024

TOTO Publishing (TOTO LTD.)
TOTO Nogizaka Bldg., 2F,
1-24-3 Minami-aoyama, Minato-ku
Tokyo 107-0062, Japan
[Sales] Telephone: +81-3-3402-7138 Facsimile: +81-3-3402-7187
[Editorial] Telephone: +81-3-3497-1010
URL: https://jp.toto.com/publishing

Authors: Koh Kitayama, Yoshiharu Tsukamoto, Ryue Nishizawa
Publisher: Akira Watai
Art Director: Hideki Nakajima
Designer: Tetsuro Furutani (Nakajima Design)
Printer: TOPPAN Colorer Inc.

Except as permitted under copyright law, this book may not be reproduced, in whole or in part, in any form or by any means, including photocopying, scanning, digitizing, or otherwise, without prior permission. Scanning or digitizing this book through a third party, even for personal or home use, is also strictly prohibited.
The list price is indicated on the cover.

ISBN 978-4-88706-312-9

Koh Kitayama

Yoshiharu Tsukamoto

Ryue Nishizawa

TOKYO METABOLIZING

目次

序文 ——————————————————————— 10
北山恒

Tokyo in Theory
21世紀初頭、東京の既成市街地のなかに見られる変容について ——— 14
北山恒

非寛容のスパイラルから抜け出すために ————————————— 28
—ヴォイド・メタボリズムにおける第4世代住宅—
塚本由晴

Tokyo in Practice: Atelier Bow-Wow
アトリエ・ワンによる第4世代の住宅 ——————————— 46
ガエ・ハウス / スウェー・ハウス / 生島文庫 /
タワーまちや / ハウス＆アトリエ・ワン
塚本由晴インタヴュー ——————————————————— 66

Tokyo in Practice: Ryue Nishizawa
森山邸—7つの新建築要素 ———————————————— 76
西沢立衛インタヴュー ——————————————————— 100

Tokyo in Practice: Koh Kitayama
洗足の連結住棟 / 祐天寺の連結住棟 ——————————— 110

結び ———————————————————————— 126
北山恒

Contents

Preface — 10
Koh Kitayama

Tokyo in Theory
Changes in Urban Areas of Tokyo at the Beginning of the 21st Century — 14
Koh Kitayama
Escaping the Spiral of Intolerance: — 28
Fourth-Generation Houses and Void Metabolism
Yoshiharu Tsukamoto

Tokyo in Practice: Atelier Bow-Wow
Fourth-Generation Houses by Atelier Bow-Wow — 46
Gae House / Sway House / Ikushima Library
Tower Machiya / House & Atelier Bow-Wow
An Interview with Yoshiharu Tsukamoto — 66

Tokyo in Practice: Ryue Nishizawa
Moriyama House: Seven New Architectural Elements — 76
An Interview with Ryue Nishizawa — 100

Tokyo in Practice: Koh Kitayama
G-Flat / Yutenji Apartments — 110

Conclusion — 126
Koh Kitayama

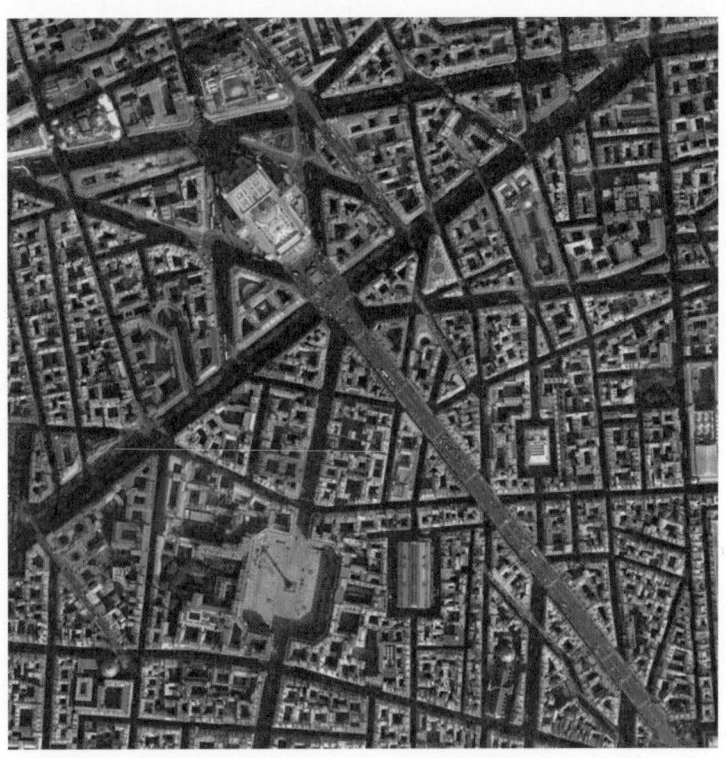

City of Monarchism

City of Capitalism

The Metabolizing City

序文

　第12回ヴェネチア・ビエンナーレ国際建築展が開催される2010年は、1960年に日本からメタボリズムという概念を発信して半世紀たつという年である。メタボリズムとは、日本が世界に向けて初めて発信した建築・都市についての影響力のあるマニフェストである。そのコンセプトは、都市を機械のように機能部品の置き換えによって新陳代謝させるという革命的なものであった。しかし、そのメガロマニアックな都市イメージは、実際には現前していない。だが、この50年間で東京の様相は凄まじい変化を遂げたことを考えれば、メタボリズムによって言語化された概念は静かに進行していたと言える。
　東京はヨーロッパで見られる連続壁体でつくられる都市構造ではなく、1つ1つが独立した建物（グレイン）の集合体として構成されている。すなわち個体の個別変容が容易に行なえるシステムを内在しているのだ。絶え間なく生成変化する独特の様相を観察していると、東京という街が「新しい建築」、そして「都市建築理論」を生み出す孵化装置であることがわかる。
　2008年の資本主義経済の大きなクラッシュの後、資本権力のアイコンとしての建築が都市の主役から退場し、生活を支える建築のあり方が問われている。都市とは経済活動の場であるのだが、同時にその空間の大部分を占めるのは生活の場である。「東京」という都市は、その都市のビジョンを決定する主体の存在は明確でないが、これまでの都市が強大な公的権力や資本権力によって形成されたのに対して、生活を中心とした静かな都市要素の変化の集積によって壮大な都市の変化を創る可能性を示している。

北山 恒

Preface

This year, during which the Venice Biennale's 12th International Architecture Exhibition will be held, marks exactly 50 years since the emergence of metabolism. This was the first influential manifesto regarding architecture and the city that had ever been transmitted from Japan to the world. The innovative concept called for the city to be metabolized by replacing its functional components as if it were a machine. But this megalomaniacal urban image hasn't come to pass. If one considers the tremendous change that Tokyo has undergone over the last half century, however, the ideas metabolism verbalized do seem to be quietly evolving.

Unlike the urban structures one finds in Europe that were created with a series of walls, Tokyo consists of an assemblage of independent buildings (grains). In other words, constant change is an inherent part of the system. In examining the unique aspects of this unceasing change, one realizes that the city of Tokyo is an incubator for new forms of architecture and urban architectural theories.

Following the huge crash of the capitalist economy in 2008, architecture lost its central urban role as an icon of financial power and a multitude of questions began to be raised concerning its ability to support our lives. Though the city is the site of economic activity, the majority of its space is taken up by living places. Whether Tokyo will take the lead in determining a new vision for the city is unclear. But in contrast to cities of the past that were shaped by tremendous administrative and financial power, Tokyo has the potential to create change in the city through the quiet accumulation of urban elements rooted in daily life.

Koh Kitayama

Tokyo in Theory

21世紀初頭、東京の既成市街地の
なかに見られる変容について
テキスト：北山恒

アイコン化する建築

　21世紀初頭、東京の街は1990年代のバブル崩壊の負債をかかえ経済の停滞期を抜け出せずにいた。また経済が不活発であったために土地価格も低く抑えられていたようである。世界の大都市のなかで東京の地価は割安感があるという話を聞いていた。同時期、この1990年代には経済のグローバリゼーションは急激に顕在化し、資本は国家の枠組みを超えて最適な位置に簡単に移動することが明らかになっていた。

　東京では、世界マーケットを対象とするスーパーブランド企業が、銀座・青山界隈に土地を購入し、旗艦店（フラッグシップ）といわれる独立店舗を競争するように建設した。エルメスは1998年に銀座5丁目の580m²の土地を100億円弱で、プラダは1999年に南青山5丁目の984m²の土地を約60億円で、ヴィトンは2000年に神宮前5丁目の577m²の土地を40億円弱で、いずれも現金一括で購入したそうである（AERA、2000年10月「ブランドに買われる日本」）。当時エルメスは、地域別売り上げシェアで、創業以来ずっとトップだったフランスを日本が抜き、その日本法人の年商は278億円であった。同時期、ヴィトンは1,357億円、プラダ・ジャパンの年商は300億円といわれ、日本が世界のスーパーブランドにとって重要な戦略的マーケットであることが明らかになっていた。プラダの日本における旗艦店であるプラダブティック青山店は、20世紀の世紀末に企画され、竣工したのは2004年である。このヘルツォーク＆ド・ムーロンの設計した、プラダブティック青山店の100億円を超えるといわれる総事業費は、当然のことながら広告宣伝費のなかですべて回収される。

　プラダブティック青山店は免震装置によって地盤からアイソレイトされ、外装の格子状の網籠そのものが構造体という建築である。構造体そのものが菱形のガラスを受けているので表層には付着した装飾という二次構成材は存在しない。というか、建物そのものが装飾（ダック）のようである。その記号性を強化するように建物周

1.
プラダブティック青山店
Prada Boutique Aoyama (2004)

Changes in Urban Areas of Tokyo at the Beginning of the 21st Century
Text: Koh Kitayama

Architecture as Icon

At the outset of the 21st century, the city of Tokyo was saddled with debts stemming from the collapse of the bubble economy in the 90s and had yet to extricate itself from financial stagnation. The sluggish economy had also suppressed land prices, and in comparison to many other large cities in the world, property had become quite reasonable. At the same time, the economic globalization of the 90s suddenly seemed to have become a reality, and capital was clearly transcending national boundaries and moving to the optimum location.

In Tokyo, fashion superbrands purchased land in the Ginza and Aoyama districts, and built flagship stores to compete with one another. In 1998, Hermes acquired a 580-square-meter lot in Ginza 5-chome for nearly ¥10 billion; in 1999, Prada bought a 984-square-meter property in Minami Aoyama 5-chome for approximately ¥6 billion; and in 2000, Louis Vuitton obtained a 577-square-meter parcel of land in Jingu-mae 5-chome for some ¥4 billion. All of these purchases were made with a single lump sum of cash (see "Burando ni kawareru Nihon" (The Brands Buy Japan), *Aera*, October 2000). At the time, Hermes' Japan sales had just overtaken those in France, which had been higher than any other region in the world since the founding of the company, and the Japanese arm of the firm had attained an annual turnover of ¥27.8 billion. During the same period, Louis Vuitton's yearly sales totaled ¥135.7 billion, and Prada Japan's topped ¥30 billion, making it abundantly clear that Japan had become an important strategic market for the world's superbrands. Plans for *Prada Boutique Aoyama*, the company's flagship store in Japan, were laid at the end of the 20th century, and construction was completed in 2004. Designed by Herzog & de Meuron, the total project cost reportedly exceeded ¥10 billion, a sum which, needless to say, was recouped through its advertising potential.

Isolated from the foundation using an anti-seismic apparatus, the exterior latticework of the "basket" functions as the structure of *Prada Boutique Aoyama*. As the structure consists of diamond-shaped sections of glass, there are no secondary components ornamenting the building's surface; or rather, the structure itself is an ornament ("duck"). To emphasize its symbolic nature, the building is surrounded by open space, beautifully isolating it from the neighborhood. A subject of great interest, the building rose up like a billboard and promptly attracted huge crowds of shoppers. The inner space of the structure, which seems to flow vertically, gives the building a theme-park-like air. Admirably satisfying the superbrand's request for something that would function as an advertisement, it is truly an outstanding design. Awarded the Architectural Institute of Japan's prize for best work, *Prada Boutique Aoyama* signals a new current in architecture.

The architecture creates an icon that is detached from the surrounding townscape. In effect, *Prada Boutique Aoyama* is a billboard for a superbrand that is completely disconnected from its physical context. The only rule the building obeys in regard to context is an imperceptible one: It is setback from the road. As it was built prior to the implementation of the sky-exposure-rate regulation, this element, which like a game makes the building rise up as one moves away from the site, undoubtedly provided the architects with hours of fun. In time, many other superbrand buildings that inspired widespread interest also appeared in Tokyo, and even in the architecture media, this was seen as an important trend. To imbue a building that is confined to a lot and can only be experienced by actually visiting the site with advertising value, several things are necessary. The site of the lot must be suited to the image of the brand, the architect(s) must also be a brand that has appeared in international competitions, and needless to say, the architecture must serve as a symbol for the brand. In contrast to the advertising medium, in which things are released and consumed in the transitory context of time, architecture is real and when it creates interest, the media automatically amplifies its value. To a superbrand, which is in the business of selling images, the investment cost of "land+architecture" makes

囲は空地がとられ、周辺の街並からはきれいにアイソレイトされている。この建築は話題性のある際だった広告塔のように出現し、多くの顧客を集めている。垂直に流れるようにつながる内部空間を体験していると、この建築そのものがテーマパークのようである。これはクライアントであるスーパーブランドが要求する広告宣伝という役割に見事に応えた、優れた建築なのだ。2005年に日本建築学会作品賞を受賞したこの建物は、建築という存在の新しい潮流を指し示していた。

　建築はアイコン化し周辺の街並から切り離される。このプラダブティック青山店は土地のコンテクストとは無関係に建つスーパーブランドの広告塔だ。唯一、この建築が場所に存在するコンテクストに対応しているのは道路斜線という眼には見えないルールであろう。まだ天空率が施行される前だったので、敷地境界から逃げれば高さが揚がるというゲームのように面白いこのルールを設計者は楽しんだに違いない。この後、東京には数多くの話題性のあるスーパーブランドの建築が生まれ、建築メディアのなかでも中心的なテーマとして扱われている。その場所に行かなければ経験できないという、土地に拘束された建築そのものに広告価値があると言うためにはいくつかの条件が必要である。立地する場所がブランドイメージに適合する土地であり、建築家も世界トーナメントに出場するブランドであること、そしてもちろん建築そのものがブランドを表象していなければならない。刹那的に時間のなかで垂れ流され消費される広告媒体に対し、建築は実在し、話題を取ればメディアがオートマティカルにその価値を増幅させる。イメージを売るスーパーブランドの企業にとって〈土地＋建築〉の投資コストはブランドイメージを構築する出費として計算が合うのである。

　このような広告塔としての建築は、立地する街のイメージは使うのだが、その街並からは切り離されていなければアイコンにはならない。アイコンとして表層が重要となるから、装飾や看板などの二次構成材を用いない。基本的にダックである。街のなかでアイコンとして認識されることが重要なので内部には無関心である。それはその内部に展示する商品がいつでも入れ替えられる必要があるし、その都度商品陳列が容易であるように、がらんとしたギャラリーのように設えられることが要求され

ているからである。外装と内部空間は無関係に自律する。だから外装だけで着ぐるみのようにつくられてアイコン建築とされることもある。日本ではヨーロッパの都市と異なり都心部でも建築物が連続体としてつくられていないので、このようなアイコニックな建築が次々と生産されているのだ。

建築を生産する社会

　20世紀初頭、ヨーロッパで始まる建築におけるモダニズム運動は、当時台頭してきた新しい市民社会に対応した建築であった。正確に言えば産業構造が変革するなかで、それ以前の社会を支配した権力セクターが退場し、それまでとは異なった新しい社会に移行した。その社会を主導する裕福な市民層（ブルジョワジー）が登場し、その市民層をクライアントとした建築のありかたが生産されたのだ。それがモダニズム運動である。それ以前の社会では建築を企図する主体は王権や宗教権力などの社会を支配する権力セクターであり、そこでは建築は権力という眼には見えないものを表象する言語として構想されていた。モダニズムの建築はそのような建築とは異なり、権力という力を表象するものではなく、逆にその力を解除した建築として構想されていたように思える。建築は新しい市民社会の生活様式＝ライフスタイルそのものを表現するものであった。モダニズムの建築はそれまでの実体としての表象ではなく、建築をメタレベルの存在に持ち込んでしまったのである。様式は無意味なものになり、建築は人間の行為に対応する装置というものになった。「住宅は住むための機械である」という過激な宣言は、新しい概念を発見した喜びに満ちている。モダニズムの建築の主役は生活する人間である。だから、形態それ自体には重要な意味を与えず、その意図を明確に伝達させるように抽象性を強化させたものである。そのためにモダニズムの建築は、周囲とは切り離されたオブジェクトとして認識されるのだが、本来的には、モダニズムに適合するライフスタイルのある場所にはどこでも再現（リプリゼンテーション）することが可能なシステムであると考えられるのだ。

　20世紀後半になるとこの社会は資本原理に回収されることが明らかになる。都市は経済行為を行う装置で

perfect sense as an expense to construct a "brand image."

As a billboard, the building makes use of the image of the area where it's located, but in order to become an icon, it must be detached from the townscape. As its surface as an icon takes on special importance, secondary components such as ornaments and signs are completely avoided. The building is fundamentally a "duck." And because its recognition as an icon in the area is essential, the building's interior is of little concern. This is related to the need to constantly change the products on display and to maintain a barren gallery-like space with racks and shelves that are simple enough to lend themselves to this task. The exterior and interior spaces are completely autonomous of each other. This is why some icon architecture is designed, like a costume, as only an exterior. Unlike European cities, even in the inner city, Japanese architectural structures aren't created as a continuum, which explains why these iconic buildings are produced in such rapid succession.

The Society That Produces Architecture

The modernist movement in architecture that began in Europe in the early 20th century corresponded to a new civil society that emerged at around the same time. To be more precise, as the industrial structure underwent a variety of changes, the state, which had dominated society in the past, withdrew, and a shift toward a different kind of society began. An affluent class of citizens (the bourgeoisie) came to lead this society, and as clients, this group determined the type of architecture that was produced. Thus began modernism. Until that point, architecture was overseen by the ruling authority, be it royal or religious, and as such, was conceived as a language that embodied an invisible power. Conversely, rather than representing the power of authority, modern architecture was conceived as something to deactivate it. Architecture began to reflect the lifestyle of this new civil society, and was no longer a symbol of entities that had existed in the past but assumed a meta-level. Style became meaningless, and architecture served as a device that corresponded directly to human activity. The radical pronouncement that "a house

2

2.
サヴォア邸
Villa Savoye (1931)

あり、都市に集合する根拠とは経済そのものになっていた。「近代世界の空間は、均質性──断片化──序列化というはっきりとした性格をもっている。この空間はさまざまな理由から均質性へと向かう傾向をもつ。同じような介入を求められる諸要因と物質の製造、管理と統御の方法、監視とコミュニケーションの方法が均質性を推し進める。均質性といっても、それは計画の均質性ではなく、構想の均質性である。人々は集合しているが、それは虚偽であり、事実上は隔離されている」（H・ルフェーブル）と記述される近代社会が要求する空間はアイソレイトしている。都市に用意される集合住宅は、遮音性能の高い界壁によって区画され、同じ規模の住戸単位が最小限の幅員をもつ共用廊下によって並べられる。その住戸単位はスチールドアで共用廊下から区画され、内部に入ると窓は無限遠に向かう。たとえ隣戸で人が殺されていてもその気配は感じられない。

　近郊の分譲住宅地では、敷地規模のそろった宅地に少しずつスキマをあけて、同じような規模の住宅が建ち並ぶ。ディベロッパーは立地によってマーケットを設定しているから、そこで扱われる住宅は同じような規模で同じような価格帯の商品となる。ここに集まり住まう人々は、マーケットセグメントされた消費者として等質な人々の集まりであるだけで、集合の理屈はその他にはない。敷地規模の小さな分譲住宅地であっても必ず一戸建てであり、その隣棟間にわずかなスキマをあけて建ち並ぶ。これは日本では1つの敷地に1つの建物しか建てられないという法律があり、外壁を敷地境界から0.5m壁面後退させなくてはならないという民法の規定があるからである。分譲住宅地では規模は均質なのだが、少しずつ色や形の違う住宅で埋め尽くされる。内藤廣がこのような風景を「意気地無しの風景」と名付けたが、同じような規模の区画割の中で、精一杯の個性を示す分譲住宅地の風景は、この国に平等な市民社会が存在し、民主主義が機能していることを表現している。と、同時にこの均質性のなかで人々は分断され孤立化しているのだ。

都市を消費するメカニズム

　1960年に提出された都市が新陳代謝して更新されていくというメタボリズムという概念は、1つの敷地に

3

4

3.
近代に開発された巨大な人間収容装置のような集合住宅
Huge housing complex developed in the modern era to function as a device for containing people.

4.
東京近郊の分譲住宅地
Housing subdivisions in the suburbs of Tokyo

is a machine for living in" was filled with the joy of discovering a new concept. The central role in modernism was played by living people. Without giving any importance to the form itself, the emphasis was placed on abstraction to clearly convey this intention. As a result, modern architecture became recognized as an art object that was detached from its surroundings, but on a fundamental level, functioned as a system that allowed a place that was conducive to a modern lifestyle to be reproduced anywhere.

By the mid-20th century, it had become clear that this society would be fueled by capitalistic principles. The city was an apparatus for conducting economic activities and the basis for people to assemble in a city was also purely economic. As Henri Lefebvre explained, modern society required isolated spaces: "The space produced by 'modernity' has specific characteristics: homogeneity—fragmentation—heirarchy. It tends towards the homogeneous for various reasons: manufacture of elements and materials (and corresponding demands on the part of those involved), methods of management and control, surveillance and communication. Homogeneity, but no plans or projects. False 'ensembles' —in fact, units. Because paradoxically (again) this homogeneous space is fragmented: lots and parcels. Reduced to crumbs! Which produced ghettos, units, clusters of detached houses [*groupes pavillonnaires*] and pseudo-schemes [*pseudo-ensembles*], poorly linked with their surroundings and with town centres." Urban housing complexes are partitioned with boundary walls that are highly effective at reducing noise, and within them, housing units of the same size are lined up along a common corridor of minimum width. The units are in turn partitioned from the corridor using steel doors, and inside, the windows point toward infinity. If someone was murdered next door, we probably wouldn't know the difference.

With a small gap between the standardized lots in suburban housing subdivisions, houses of the same size line the streets. As developers control the market through location, the houses they deal with in any given area are products of the same size in the same price range. Other than the fact that the people who assemble in these areas are part of the same consumer-based market segment, there is little

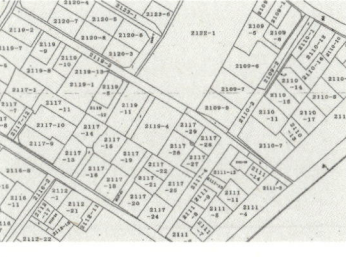

5

6

5.
細分化された土地所有の区画図
Diagram of subdivided land

6.
1敷地1建物システムによって建物は容易に取り替え可能である
The one-structure, one-lot system makes it easy to replace buildings.

1つずつ建築が建てられる、というこのシステムによって実現されている。一定のスキマをもって建築が建ち並ぶ日本の都市風景は、遠景すれば色鮮やかで均質なグレインのカーペットに見える。それは周囲との関係性を必要としない勝手気ままなフリースタンディングの建築物の集合である。日本の建築のライフサイクルが短いのは、その変化を担保する社会システムが存在するからである。日本の都市は同じような規模の建物がショーケースに陳列されるショートケーキのように建ち並ぶ。都市は〈土地＋建物〉がセットとなった区分可能な商品の集合である。そしてそれぞれの商品はショーケースのなかで少しでも高価に見えるように身体をくねらせ精一杯周囲との差異化を図る。都市の構成要素である小建築も区分可能な商品としてアイコニックに変容しているのだ。ヨーロッパでは日本のマンガとともにこのカワイイ日本のアイコン建築はブームである。

21世紀に入って都市再生特別措置法による容積率の緩和などが矢継ぎ早に打ち出され、東京の湾岸地域にはタワーマンションが林立し始めている。今後200本ほど計画されているそうだが、計画地はほとんどが工場跡地などの産業用地である。湾岸地区の大型の産業用地であった敷地が、産業構造の変化に従って高収益を上げるタワーマンションの計画地となっているのだ。もともと工業地域で生活をサポートする施設のないエリアだから、このタワーマンションは周囲とは無関係に敷地内で自己完結した計画となる。100年後にはスラムになると言われるタワーマンションが、隣接しながら互いには無関係に自律し、増殖を続ける。このタワーマンションもアイコンとして認識される新しい都市のプレイヤーである。日本の都市を構成するあらゆる建築は資本ゲームの取り替え可能なコマなのだ。そして、このようにして日本の都市風景は簡単に更新されていく。

敷地の拘束を超えていくもの

現実の社会では建築を構想することは必ず敷地に拘束されている。しかし、あたりまえのことながら大学の研究課題では敷地を容易に越境することができる。数年前、私の教える大学の大学院で「アーバンヴォイドプログラム」という都市研究をおこなった。それは、「日本

7

8

7.
メタボリズムのプロジェクト：海上都市1963／菊竹清訓
Metabolist architecture project:
Marine City 1963 by Kiyonori Kikutake

8.
林立するタワーマンション
Forest of tower blocks

reason for them to be together. Despite the small lots, the houses are invariably detached and lined up side-by-side with a narrow gap between them. In Japan, this is due to an ordinance stipulating that only one structure can be built on a lot, and a civil law that requires the exterior wall to be set 0.5 meters back from the edge of the lot. Though the size of the houses is the same in a subdivision, there is a vast range of subtly different colors and shapes. Hiroshi Naito has described this type of landscape as "spineless," but a subdivision that has done its utmost to express its individuality within plots of land of the same size, is indicative of the fact that an egalitarian civil society and a functioning democracy exist in Japan. Yet, at the same time, within this standardized community, people remain divided and isolated.

A Mechanism for Consuming the City

The city proposed in the 1960s was realized according to a system, based on the concept of metabolism or renewal, in which each structure was built on a single lot. From a distance, the urban landscape of Japan, lined with these structures separated by a fixed gap, had the appearance of a carpet composed of brilliant, homogeneous grains. This resulted in a collection of free-willed, free-standing architectural structures without any relation to their surroundings. The short life-cycle of Japanese architecture is said to stem from a social system that guarantees change. In a Japanese city, structures of the same size are displayed like pieces of shortcake in a showcase. The city is a collection of divisible products that come in a set of "land+structure." And in order to make each of the items in the showcase appear to be a little more valuable, a mind-numbing effort is made to differentiate them from their surroundings. The small structures that serve as the basic components of the city also assume an iconic status as divisible products. And along with manga, the icon architecture of *kawaii*(cute) Japan is currently enjoying a boom in Europe.

In the 21st century, following the passage of the Special Measures Concerning Urban Regeneration Act, regulations, such as those concerning floor-space ratio, were suddenly eased and a forest of tower blocks began to spring up around Tokyo Bay. With 200 more such buildings slated for the future, the zone was for the most part industrial land that originally housed factories. In other words, the area has been turned into a site for highly profitable apartment blocks in the wake of a series of changes in the country's industrial structure. As the blocks are located in a former industrial area that lacks the facilities needed in daily life, the development is self-contained and lacks any relation to its surroundings. The apartments, which some have predicted will be a slum in 100 years' time, are autonomous structures which while adjacent to each other remain disconnected and simply continue to multiply. The various structures that comprise Japanese cities are like replaceable pieces in a money game; and as such, are a simple means of renewing the urban landscape of the country.

Transcending the Confines of a Lot

In a real society, architectural conception is necessarily confined to a physical lot. As the subject of university research, however, this limitation is easily transcended. Several years ago at the Graduate School of Yokohama National University, where I teach, a research project called the "Urban Void Program" was launched. The project is based on the idea that "the grains in a market segment of dense sections of wooden houses in any Japanese urban area are more or less identical. Though the lots are narrowly segmented, as a result of the building-coverage regulation, there is a uniform rate of sky exposure. There are also gaps in these spaces that are not large enough to call a garden in which people have planted greenery. If one views the gaps and open land that were produced by the one-structure, one-lot regulation and civic code stipulating setback walls as a single network of continuous space, this wooden-housing area might be seen as a porous cluster containing garden plants. When human beings are added to the cluster, an unexpected breeze blows through the gaps, and a comfortable space in which gentle sunlight passes through the trees emerges. This spatial form may be related to the humid, temperate climate of the monsoon region. By focusing on negative space (the

の都市部にある木造密集市街地は、マーケットのセグメントが働きグレインはその地域の中ではほぼ同じである。敷地は小さく細分化されるのだが、建坪率が効いているために空地率は一定である。そこでは庭とは呼べないスキマのように残る空地が存在し、そんな空地にも庭木が植えられている。この1敷地1建物という制度と民法上の壁面後退によって生まれる、都市のなかのスキマや空地を、連続する空間のネットワークであるとして見てみると、この木造密集市街地は密度がそろい庭木を抱き込んだポーラスな塊のように認識される。そのポーラスな塊に身体を入れると、その隙間から思いがけない風が流れてきたり、庭木を通して優しい陽射しが射してくるような心地よい空間がある。それは湿度が高く温暖なモンスーン地帯に対応した空間形式であるのかもしれない。この『アーバンヴォイドプログラム』では、計画する実体としてのポジティブスペースではない、その対称にあるネガティブ・スペース（実体の建物を主体としてみたときに取り残される空間）に注目することで、分断されている住戸を編み込むような新しい空間組成が創造できる」というものである。

　大学では継続して、敷地の拘束を越えて「都市組成を編み込む装置」のようなものを開発することをテーマとしてスタディしている。ここでいう「装置」とは、「アーバンヴォイドプログラム」では都市内にあるスキマや空地のネットワークであった。さらに、社会システムの変化によって機能を失い捨て去られた残地を対象としたり、利用価値が見いだせないものを見方を変えることで有意味のものに変換させるというものである。そしてそこで発見されるものは、人がそこにいる意味を見い出し、場所に帰属感をもつ何かである。それを「都市の環境単位（socio-environmental unit）」と名付けていて、この「環境単位」というものそのものを定義しようという作業をこの数年続けている。

共同体を要請する空間

　2006年の1年間、ある建築専門誌の建築評欄を担当していた。それは年間を通して、発表される建築を全て克明に読んでいくという作業である。この一連の建築を「アーバンヴォイドプログラム」で用いた概念で読み返してみると、同じ思想によって建築概念が提出されて

アーバンヴォイドプログラム 2004-2005
Urban Void Program 2004-2005

9

10

11

9.
現状
Present state

10.
建物の粒（グレイン）の変換
Transformation of buildings (grains)

11.
空き地（ヴォイド）の変換
Transformation of empty spaces (void)

space that remains when the architectural structure is viewed as the core) rather than the positive space of the actual entity in the Urban Void Program, it is possible to create new spatial components that can be linked to a dwelling under analysis."

This study, dealing with the development of a "device to link urban components" which transcends the confines of a lot, is ongoing at the university. The "device" in this case refers to the network of gaps and open spaces within the city that was examined in the Urban Void Program. In addition, a special effort has been made to focus on land that has lost its function and been abandoned due to changes in the social system, and through the adoption of new perspectives, give new meaning to land that has been deemed to have no utility value. What researchers have discovered in the process is that when people derive meaning from being in a certain place, they develop a sense of belonging. And over the last few years, work has continued to try and define the "environmental unit" (referred to as a "socio-environmental unit") itself.

Spaces Calling Out for a Community

For one year, in 2006, I wrote a book review column in a certain architecture magazine. The job entailed meticulously reading every book on architecture that was published during that period. Reexamining them in the context of the Urban Void Program, I realized that architectural concepts are all part of the same sort of thinking. *House & Atelier Bow-Wow* may be a small structure but it contains an important message: By valuing the various negative spaces that exist in the city and equating them with actual spaces, it is possible to create a completely new space (third space). Residual spaces such as gaps and windows that open wide in the direction of the adjacent land allow the area that extends as far as the exterior wall of the neighboring house to function as one's own territory. At the same time, the existence of a gap inevitably leads to a relationship with the other house. In that sense, a meaning unlike that of the past seems to have been assigned to residual space in the city. Displaying an even more clear-cut strategy, *Moriyama House* dismantles the concept of the lot. By

12.

12.
都市の外部空間を再構成する提案
Proposal for restructuring external urban spaces

いるものがあることに気づく。ハウス＆アトリエ・ワンは小さな建築であるがとても重要なメッセージが込められていた。都市に存在するさまざまなネガティブ・スペースを積極的に評価して、それと実空間を同一化し、そこから全く新しい空間（第3空間）として立ち上げようと意図されていることがわかる。隣地に向けて大きくあいた開口はスキマのように存在する残余空間を通して、隣家の外壁までを自らの領域に取り込んでいる。と、同時に、そのスキマの存在によって隣家との関係は抜き差しならないものに持ち込まれている。ここでは都市のなかの残余スペースに、それまでとは異なる意味が与えられているようである。そして森山邸はさらに明快な戦略をもって敷地の概念を解体している。計画する建築そのものに、多様な空隙のような外部空間を抱き込むことで、周囲の街のなかに存在する微細な外部空間と連続し、その環境のなかに同一化している。ここでは実空間とその実空間によって切り取られた残余空間が等価に扱われているようにみえるのだが、さらには主体がこの残余空間であり、まるで実空間は残余空間のためにあるように読み取ることもできる。そして、この空隙のネットワークによって諸室は濃密に関係させられ、集合して住むというプログラムを強化していることがわかる。ここでは新しい建築の規範が生み出されているのだ。

　この2つの建築は敷地の拘束を解除する方策を、概念（他の敷地を侵犯せずに）として指し示していた。ともに生活に関係するプログラムであることに注意する必要がある。そして、上述のハウス＆アトリエ・ワンと森山邸と同時期に私が設計していた洗足の連結住棟では、通常の計画手法では大きなヴォリュームとなる一棟建築を解体して分割すること、その分割によって生まれる残余空間をもう1つの主要な計画対象と考えたものである。透明な住戸はこのネガティブ・スペースによって住戸間相互の関係をつけるのだが、それは互いの生活の気配を否応なく感じるものであり、そのため相互の心遣いと配慮が要求されるというものである。このように東京では同じ時期に同様の計画概念をもつ住居が構想されていたことが興味深い。このコンセプトを展開した、祐天寺の連結住棟では、さらに複雑に内部空間と外部空間を相互浸透させている。

　このような計画概念が提出されているのは、生活に

13

14

13.
ハウス＆アトリエ・ワン
House & Atelier Bow-Wow (2005)

14.
森山邸
Moriyama House (2005)

enfolding various void-like exterior spaces into the architectural plan itself, the work continues into the subtle exterior space of the surrounding area, and is assimilated into the environment. Here, the actual space and the residual space that is detached by means of the actual space seem to be treated equally. Moreover, the core is the residual space, and the actual space seems to exist on its behalf. Through this network of voids, a rich connection is created between the various rooms in the house, clearly emphasizing the program of assembling and living. In effect, the work marks the birth of a new scale of architecture.

The strategy in these two works of architecture is to dissolve the limits of the lot and present a concept (without interfering with the other lots). At the same time, one should note that the program relates to living. In both *House & Atelier Bow-Wow* and *Moriyama House* as well as my own *G-Flat*, designed during the same period, by dismantling and dividing a single structure that would occupy a large volume using ordinary methods of planning, the residual space that emerged as a result of the work came to be another important target in the project. Through this negative space, the transparent dwelling came to have a reciprocal relationship with the neighboring dwellings, but rather than forcing the residents to acknowledge each other's presence, the works call for mutual regard and consideration. It's interesting to think that the houses were all conceived according to similar plans in the same era in the city of Tokyo. In my work, *Yutenji Apartments*, I developed this concept even further, creating an even more complex level of mutual permeance between the interior and the exterior.

In conceiving a space for living, this type of planning concept has its limitations in terms of managing the public/private dichotomy, which in contemporary society, clearly leads to the further isolation of space. But adopting the dichotomy of the broader concept of commons vs. market, which was first actualized in a capital-based society in the mid-20th century, as a topic of investigation, verifies whether or not the structure of the new space can be developed.

In apartment complexes developed during the

15

16

15.
洗足の連結住棟
G-Flat (2006)

16.
祐天寺の連結住棟
Yutenji Apartments (2010)

対応する空間を構想するなかで、パブリック／プライベートという二項対立でその計画を管理することには限界があり、現代の社会ではそれがさらに空間の孤立を進行させていることが明らかだからである。そこでは、20世紀後半から資本を中心とした社会のなかに顕在しているコモンズ／マーケットという上位概念としての対立項を検討の項目に組み入れることで、新しい空間の構成が展開できるか検証されているのだ。

近代に開発された集合住宅は、同じような規模の単位空間が共用廊下に接続して並べられ、住戸内に入ると窓からの視線は無限遠に向かい隣戸の様子はうかがえない。人間の生活は管理され、隔離された人々が収容される容器のようである。それに対して既成市街地の木造密集地区では、家と家との間のスキマのような、所有の重なる外部空間が存在し、否応なく身体がぶつかり、お互いの視線が交差する。そこでは、身体をもった人間がお互いの動作に思いやり気遣わなくてはならない。互いの関係性を決定する行為の主体が人間にあるため、人間を管理するという意図は成立しないのである。そして、このような関係性の存在が、共同体であることを意識せざるを得ない空間を生成するものなのだ。

新しい建築そして都市

このように温暖なモンスーン気候帯にある東京では、年間を通じて外部空間が心地よい期間が長いので、内部空間と外部空間が相互に浸透し、公的な空間から最も私的な空間へ視線が通る透明性の高い住居空間が存在する。このような開放系の空間では、プライバシーを計画原理とする近代主義の集合形式ではない住まい方が存在するのだ。この数年、このような集合形式を肯定的に評価した新しい住居が提案され、それが実現され、経験されている。人々はこの自在に相互の人間関係をつくれる解放区のような集合体を選択している。

2008年の資本主義経済の大きなクラッシュの後、資本権力のアイコンとしての建築が都市の主役からしだいに退場し、生活を支える建築のあり方が問われている。都市とは経済活動の場であるのだが、同時にその都市の大多数を占める主役は生活の場である。それは、生活をする人間の側に主体があり、人間の集合形式に根拠を与える空間である。集まって生活することの根拠（＝都市の存在理由）こそ現代の社会が真剣に必要としている事柄なのだ。東京では生活を支えるための住居という都市の最小の構成単位のあり方が、その最適解を求めて絶えず変容している。この都市は、強大な権力や資本の対極にある、単位住居という小さな個人的な事柄によって、壮大な都市の再編成が行われるのかもしれない。

modern era, unit spaces of the same size were connected and lined up along a common corridor, and the line of sight from the windows inside the dwelling extended infinitely outward without a glimpse of the scene next door. These units were like vessels that controlled human life and contained isolated people. Conversely, in the dense sections of wooden houses in an urban area, there is a jointly owned external space resembling a gap between two houses in which bodies are forced to collide and glances are exchanged. Here, human beings with a physical form must unexpectedly give thought to each other's movements. As the central roles in an act that determines the relationship between them is played by human beings, the intention to control each other never arises. And the existence of this type of relationship produces a space in which people are made aware of the fact that they are part of a community.

New Architecture and the City

As exterior spaces remain comfortable in Tokyo, with its temperate, monsoon climate, for a good portion of the year, interior and exterior spaces tend to permeate each other, and many living spaces possess a high degree of transparency through which the line of sight passes from a public space to the most private space. In this type of open space, one finds a way of living that didn't exist in the modern collective form that valued privacy as a planning principle. In recent years, this open form has been affirmed and as new housing proposals are submitted, the concept is becoming more widely realized and experienced. People are selecting collective dwellings with open areas that can be adjusted to create personal relationships with each other.

Following the crash of the capitalist economy in 2008, architecture, as an icon of financial authority, has gradually receded from its central role in the city, and the state of architecture as a means of supporting daily life has come to be reexamined. The city is a site of economic activity, but at the same time, the majority of spaces in it are related to living. In other words, the main focus is on the people who live in the city, and the spaces are based on the notion of collective forms for them. A basis for collective living (=the reason for the existence of a city) is something for which there is a serious need in contemporary society. The state of the city's smallest structural units, the houses which support people's lives in Tokyo, is undoubtedly changing in order to provide the optimum solutions. Through the small, personal matter of dwelling units, the city, with its dual extremes of massive authority and capital, seems to be undergoing a grand reorganization.

非寛容のスパイラルから抜け出すために
——ヴォイド・メタボリズムにおける第4世代住宅——
テキスト：塚本由晴

　東京は戸建て住宅でできた都市と言える程、びっしりとその地表を住宅で埋め尽くされている。その住宅は、1920年以降の郊外の住宅地開発にあわせて生まれた、いわゆる近代家族に対応した戸建て住宅の系譜にあり、2010年の今年はその90年目にあたる。そういう日本の戸建て住宅の平均寿命は26年である。単純計算しても過去に2回の建て替えがあってもおかしくはない。この90年間の日本社会は真に激しく変化した。建設技術、材料、法規、経済、家族など、住宅の背景になるものが、約90年でどれほど変わったことか。もちろん住宅の寿命には個体差があるから、実際には第1世代から第3世代までの住宅がランダムに入り交じって建っている。多世代の住宅が混在する風景は、言い換えればこうした社会背景の違いを同時に見せられているようなものである。そう考えれば、東京の風景がよく「混沌」と形容されるのも、この「住宅寿命26年」という周期を内蔵しつつ、新陳代謝＝メタボリズムを繰り返しているからである。

　しかしその姿は、60年代のメタボリズムが想像したものとはずいぶん違ったものになっている。60年代のそれは、資本や権力の集中によって都市が建設されていくことを疑わなかった不変のコアと可変のカプセルの組み合わせによってモデル化されていた。しかし今我々が関わっているメタボリズムは、住宅の1粒1粒が、個人所有者のイニシアチブによって、隙間（ヴォイド）をつねに保ちながら入れ替わっていくものだから、都市空間の実践における資本と権力は徹底的に分散されており、その意味で民主主義の都市風景と言えなくもない。また税金をほとんど使わなくても、住環境として維持されていくという意味では、形式としての持続性が高いと言える。これを60年代のコアに象徴されるメタボリズムに対して、「ヴォイド・メタボリズム」と呼んでみたい。

　ちなみにイギリスの住宅の寿命は100年である。これは社会基盤である様々なインフラストラクチャーと同じ周期である。これに対して商業的な施設やファッションは5年や半年などずっと短周期であり、いわゆる移ろいゆく都市現象と言える。このためイギリスでは都市は住宅を含む変わらない社会基盤と、その上に移ろいゆく都市現象の二極にわけることで構造化できる。東京の住宅寿命26年というのは、ちょうどこの二極の間に差し込まれた、中間的な周期なのである。このために短周期の商業やファッションの活動が、都市空間のあり

1.
住宅でできた都市、東京
Tokyo, City of Houses

Escaping the Spiral of Intolerance: Fourth-Generation Houses and Void Metabolism
Text: Yoshiharu Tsukamoto

Residential sections of Tokyo were developed primarily as detached houses, and all available urban real estate has long since been completely exploited. A product of suburban housing developments begun in 1920s, the houses are part of a lineage that corresponds to the so-called "modern family" and this year, 2010, marks their 90th anniversary. The life expectancy of a Japanese house is 26 years. Simple arithmetic suggests that many of them may have been rebuilt at least twice. This 90-year period in Japanese society has seen dramatic changes. Building technologies, materials, legal frameworks, economics and the changing structure of the family have also seen important changes, but how much have these things changed in the last approximately 90 years? Of course, this may vary according to the lifespan of individual buildings, but at present there is actually a random mixture of houses that range from first- to third-generation. A landscape in which multiple generations of houses are combined indicates various changes in the social backdrop. With this in mind, one reason the Tokyo landscape is often described as "chaotic" is due to this inherent cycle of 26 years and the repeated occurrence of metabolism.

The form of contemporary Tokyo is quite different from what was envisioned by the Metabolist movement of the 1960s. The model that was advanced in the 60s presented a permanent core with variable capsules in a city that was constructed by a concentration of capital and authority. However, in the metabolism with which we are presently concerned, due to the fact that each grain or house both constantly maintains and replaces a gap (void) though the initiative of the individual owner, the capital and authority at work in the urban space is thoroughly dispersed, and Tokyo can be seen as an urban landscape of democracy. In addition, as almost no tax revenue is required to maintain this residential environment, it is a highly sustainable form. To differentiate our concept from the metabolism of the 60s, which was symbolized by the core, we would like to refer to this phenomenon as a "void metabolism."

It's interesting to note that the lifespan of a British house is 100 years. This cycle is comparable to the infrastructure that underlies the city. By comparison, commercial facilities and fashions have a much shorter cycle (in some cases, six months; in others, five years), an "ephemeral" cycle. As a result, in England, the city can be viewed in terms of a bipolar structure of an unchanging social foundation, which includes houses, and short-term urban phenomena which unfold within it. The 26-year rebuilding cycle functions between these two poles. Thus, the short cycles of commercial and fashion activity can easily be absorbed into the state of the urban space, and by influencing the surface of the city, is a phenomenon produced by void metabolism. Any attempt to adapt the urban principles of Tokyo, which give rise to these phenomena, and force them to fit a European or American model is, to be blunt, utter nonsense. Rather, consider Tokyo as an excellent urban model that ranks with the Paris of the 19th century or the New York of the early 20th century. Above all, through its in-built cycle of housing renovation, the embodiment of the changing city is one of Tokyo's most distinctive characteristics. In the 21st century, should Tokyo strive to reach greater heights as a city with this cycle intact? If so, to realize such a goal, there are several things that need to be reexamined.

One of the problems that must first be cited regarding urban space is that individual structures have simply accumulated in a quantitative manner. Unfortunately, unlike the ancient cities of Italy, there is neither a concentration of structures representing a specific architectural type in Tokyo, nor is there an organic relationship to the urban form that has taken shape there. This is partly due to earthquakes, war damage, and rapid economic growth, which have destroyed the older layers of the city, and also to the fact that modern Tokyo is still in its infancy. In addition, prior to attaining intelligence as a city, a policy of encouraging limited-plot, large-scale developments was undertaken in the name of "urban renaissance" during the administration of Prime Minister Junichiro Koizumi around 2000. In examining this formative process, it becomes clear that this form allows for void metabolism. Only,

方に吸い上げられやすくなって、都市の表層をこんなにも左右することになるのも、ヴォイド・メタボリズムが引き起こす現象の一部である。こうした現象を生み出す東京の都市の原理を、無理矢理ヨーロッパ型、あるいはアメリカ型に修正して行くべきだと考えるのは、もはやナンセンスだろう。むしろ19世紀のパリ、20世紀初頭のニューヨークに匹敵する卓越した都市モデルに、東京はなりかけていると考えた方がよい。何よりも住宅の更新周期を内蔵することによって、変化する都市を体現していることは東京の大きな特徴になっている。この周期を内蔵したまま、都市としての卓越に至ることが、21世紀の東京が目指すべき姿ではないだろうか。その実現に向けて、いくつか見直さなければならぬことが確実にある。

　まず都市空間の問題としては、それが個々の建築の単なる量的集積になってしまっていることがあげられる。残念ながら現在の東京には、イタリアの古い都市のように特定の建築類型の集積が、そのまま都市形態を形成するような有機的な関係はない。これには震災、戦災、高度経済成長などによって、都市の古層が破壊され、いまだに幼年期にあることも関係するだろう。そんなまだ都市としての知性が生まれる前に2000年頃の小泉政権下ではアーバンルネッサンスという枠組みによって大規模開発が起こっている。その成立プロセスを見ればこれもヴォイド・メタボリズムが可能にする形態であることが理解できるだろう。ただしそれは都市ではなく巨大なミニ開発であり、更新可能性を議論の外におくことでヴォイド・メタボリズムのなかでの硬直した部分となっていくだろう。けれどもこのままでは都市を相手にする知性が生まれることはない。すなわち文化資本にはなりえない。もっと部分どうしが関係しあって全体の質が決まっていくような、建築から都市までが連続する有機的な空間にできないだろうか。だが都市の端がどこにあるかわからないぐらい拡大しているので、そもそも個別の建築的投機が、その響きを確かめられるような都市の全体を捉える事ができない。そこで果てしなく続くように思われる東京の都市空間から限定的な領域を取り出し、これを中間単位として、1つ1つの建築の振る舞いとの響きを検討していく作業が必要となる。

　21世紀の今、東京の住宅地にはこれまでとは違う

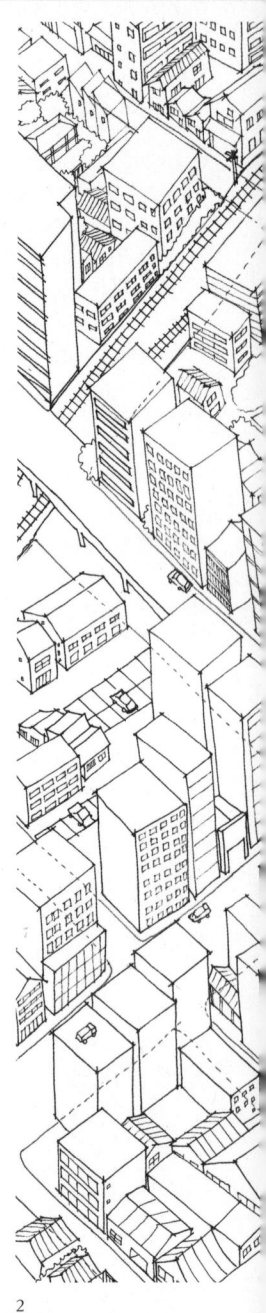

2.
ヴォイド・メタボリズムの生態系
The Void Metabolism Ecosystem

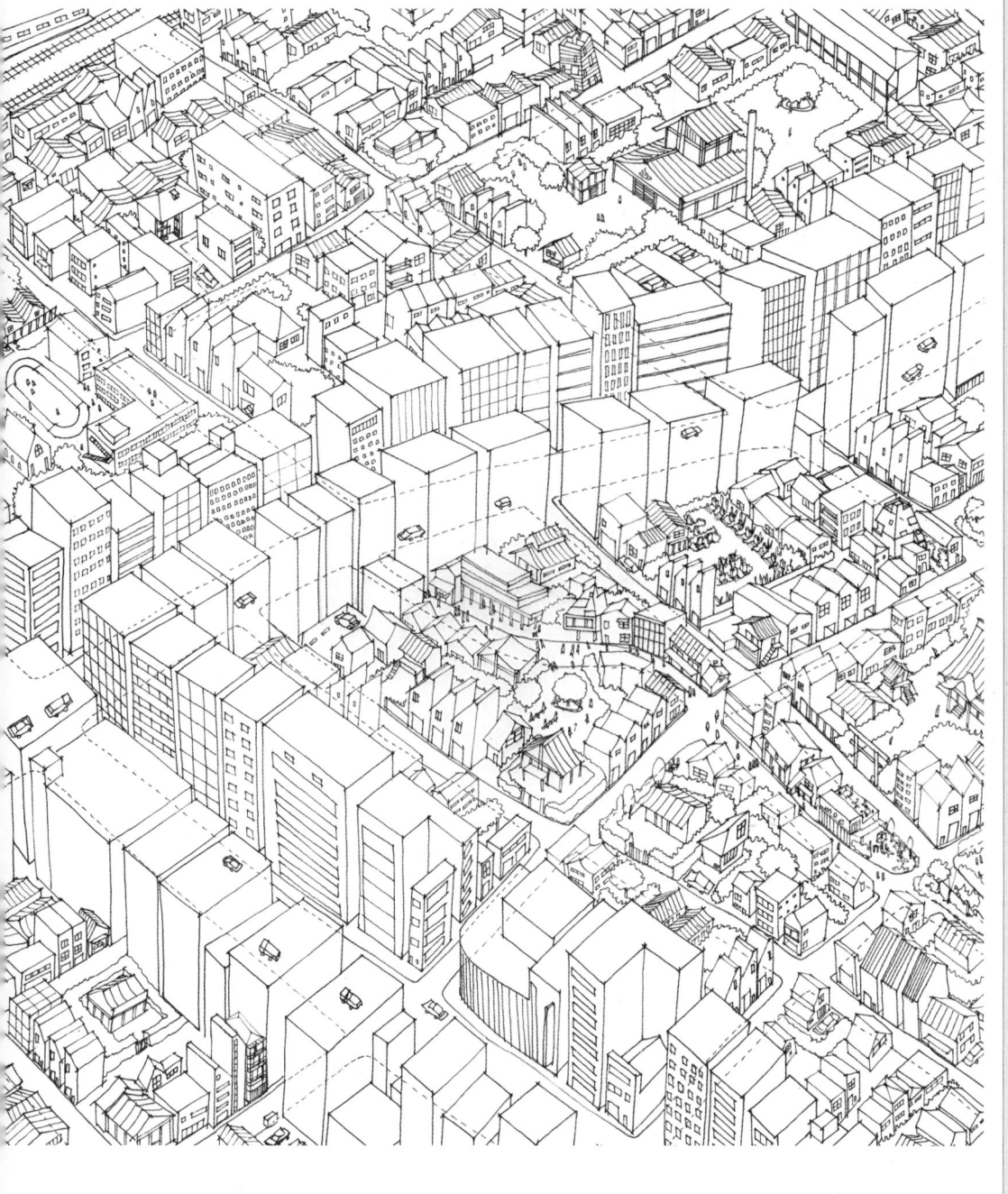

状況が訪れている。もちろん郊外への新しい開発は続けられているが、違うのは既に完成されていた住宅地が様々に変容を遂げていることである。たとえば、防災軸の設定によって10階建ての耐火建築による都市的な場所と、2階建ての住宅地による村のような場所が、カワとアンコのような関係で対比的に組み合わさっていたり(アーバンヴィレッジ)、原宿のように住宅地だったところに商業活動が入り込んでパブリックとプライベートの境界があいまいになってきたり(コマージデンス)、20世紀の前半に開発された奥沢など第1世代の郊外が拡張する都市に飲み込まれ、世帯の世代交代や不動産投資によって、細分化・高密化したり(サブディバーバン)、といった都市形態のパタンが発生している。こうしたパタンは既存の住宅が粒毎に更新されるという時間的条件の中で紡ぎ出された中間単位というものである。これら中間単位のなかで建物の群れを見ると、1つ1つ取り出してみれば個別的で統一感のない住宅に、一定の振る舞いが認められる。この群れとして浮上する振る舞いを批判的に展開させることによって、個別の住宅設計においても都市空間に対して責任ある、一貫したアプローチが可能になるであろう。

rather than urban development, this is a huge mini-development, and placing the potential for renewal outside the scope of discussion forms the rigid part within void metabolism. This alone will not produce the intelligence needed to deal with the city; it won't create cultural capital. Isn't there a way that the original elements can be connected and a continuous organic space can influence the overall quality the architecture to the city? As the city has become so vast, no one is entirely sure where it ends anymore, and it's nearly impossible to ascertain what sort of effect individual architectural speculation has had on the city as a whole. Therefore, it is necessary to extract a limited area from the seemingly endless urban fabric of Tokyo, and using this as an intermediate unit, investigate the influence that each structure exerts on the others.

Today, in the 21st century, new phenomena have appeared in Tokyo's residential areas. Of course, new development continues in the suburbs, but now existing residential areas are also displaying a variety of changes. These include, for example, the emergence of specific urban forms such as areas where ten-story, fire-resistant buildings which are part of a designated fire-belt combine with a village-like area of two-story dwellings in a pastry-like "crust-and-filling"-type of relationship ("urban village"); areas in which the border between public and private has been blurred after commercial activity increases in places such as Harajuku, which were originally residential ("commersidence"); and first-generation suburbs such as Okusawa (developed during the 1920s) that have been surrounded by expanding urbanization, and due to demographic changes and inheritance taxes, and real-estate investment, are being subdivided and growing increasingly crowded ("subdivurban"). These patterns are intermediate units that emerge within the temporal condition of renovating preexisting houses grain by grain. When one looks at the clusters of structures within these intermediate units, one notices a certain set of behaviors in the houses, which seem to be highly individual and lack any sense of unity. By developing the behavior that arises out of these groups in a critical way, wouldn't it be possible to arrive at a responsible, consistent approach to urban space through the design of individual houses?

アーバンヴィレッジ

　東京都心部では、幹線道路沿い両側30mが高容積の商業地域に指定され、中層の耐火建造物への建替えが誘導されることで、木造を含む低層の住宅群を街区内に取り囲む都市形態が見られる。「カワとアンコ」と通称されるこの形態では、幹線道路から一歩街区内に踏み込むとそこには静かな低層住宅密集地が広がることとなる。そこは庭木があふれ、細く曲がりくねった路地が多く、歩行者が道の真ん中を歩くまるで村のような環境になっていることから、私たちはこれをアーバンヴィレッジと呼んでいる。

　東京都区部ではこうした都市形態が37か所において観測される。特に新宿区内は、環状4号線（外苑西通り）、5号線（明治通り）沿いに土地区画整理事業の行われていない木賃アパートの密集する「木賃ベルト地帯」と呼ばれるエリアが数多く存在する。このエリアはM8規模の大地震によって24時間以内に燃え尽きると言われている脆弱なエリアとなっている。そのため、1995年「東京都防災都市づくり推進計画」に基づいて産業商業地域に指定されている幹線道路の多くが「骨格防災軸」に指定され、密集住宅地の延焼を塞き止める都市の防火壁としての「任務」が与えられることになった。

Urban Village

In the heart of Tokyo, 30-meter stretches of main roads were designated as high-capacity commercial zones, and due to reconstruction projects in which mid-rise, fire-resistant structures were erected, an urban form arose in which clusters of wooden houses are walled-in. In this dumpling-like form, by merely stepping off a main road and into this older neighborhood, one discovers a quiet expanse of densely packed lowrise houses. These areas are teeming with greenery, and due to the predominance of narrow, winding alleyways, there is no through traffic. This village-like atmosphere led us to call it an "urban village."

In Shinjuku in particular, there are no Land Readjustment Act projects underway, but one finds numerous so-called "*mokuchin* house belts" (densely-packed, wooden rental apartments) lining Circular Route No. 4 and Route No. 5. It has been estimated that a magnitude-8 earthquake would cause this extremely vulnerable area to burn to the ground within 24 hours. As a result, many main roads in such commercial zones have been designated as a "principal disaster reduction network" under the 1995 Development Plan for Disaster Prevention, and in return for a higher floor-area ratio along the roads, these buildings have been entrusted with the function of an urban firewall that prevents the spread of fire in crowded residential areas.

PRINCIPAL DISASTER REDUCTION NETWORK
app. 3-4km mesh

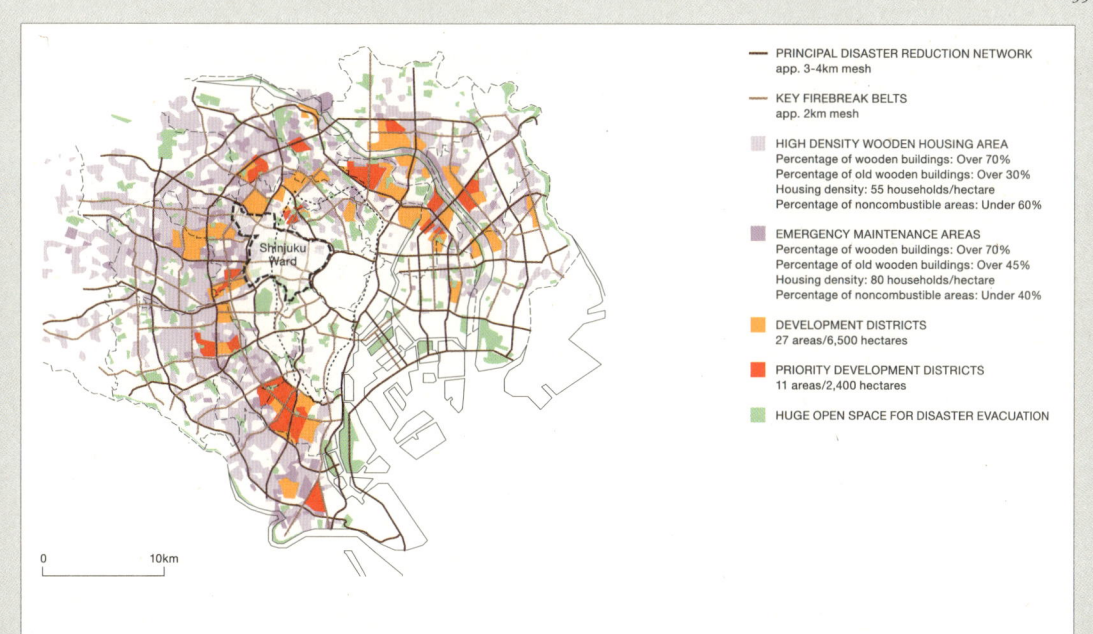

KEY FIREBREAK BELTS
app. 2km mesh

HIGH DENSITY WOODEN HOUSING AREA
Percentage of wooden buildings: Over 70%
Percentage of old wooden buildings: Over 30%
Housing density: 55 households/hectare
Percentage of noncombustible areas: Under 60%

EMERGENCY MAINTENANCE AREAS
Percentage of wooden buildings: Over 70%
Percentage of old wooden buildings: Over 45%
Housing density: 80 households/hectare
Percentage of noncombustible areas: Under 40%

DEVELOPMENT DISTRICTS
27 areas/6,500 hectares

PRIORITY DEVELOPMENT DISTRICTS
11 areas/2,400 hectares

HUGE OPEN SPACE FOR DISASTER EVACUATION

23区における延焼遮断帯、整備地域、木造住宅密集地域、避難場所を重ねた地図（東京都都市整備局の資料をもとに作成）
Map Showing Fire Belts, Development Areas, Areas with a High Concentration of Wooden Houses, and Evacuation Sites in the 23 Municipalities of Tokyo (Based on information from the Bureau of Urban Development, Tokyo Metropolitan Government)

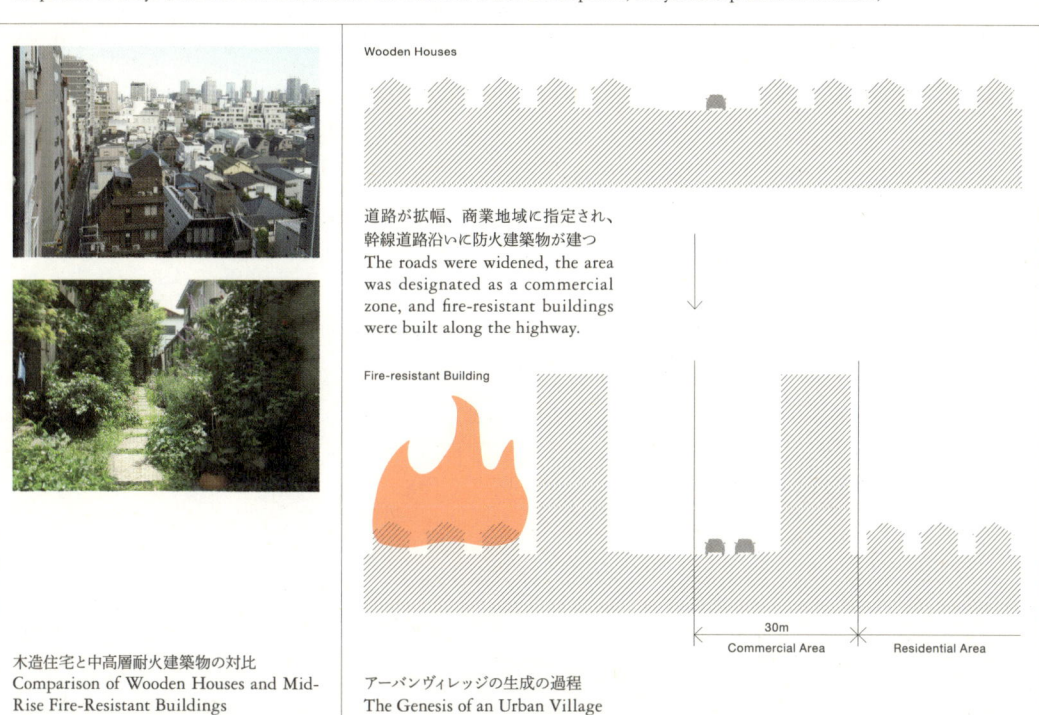

木造住宅と中高層耐火建築物の対比
Comparison of Wooden Houses and Mid-Rise Fire-Resistant Buildings

Wooden Houses

道路が拡幅、商業地域に指定され、幹線道路沿いに防火建築物が建つ
The roads were widened, the area was designated as a commercial zone, and fire-resistant buildings were built along the highway.

Fire-resistant Building

30m
Commercial Area Residential Area

アーバンヴィレッジの生成の過程
The Genesis of an Urban Village

コマージデンス

　　コマージデンスとは住居地域に隣接する商業地域の活動が侵入していくパタンのことである。生活排水の流入による汚染のひどかった渋谷川は、1964年の東京オリンピックを機会に都市計画道路に指定され暗渠化されたが、当初は接道条件が満たされないために建替えのきかない小さな住宅（第1世代）の間を抜ける遊歩道であった。80年代になると住宅を改造した古着屋など（第2世代）が点在し始め「キャットストリート」と呼ばれるようになる。1996年の道路拡張に伴い沿道の敷地が建築可となると、まず計画道路にかかる敷地に鉄骨3階建ての店舗（第3世代）ができ始め、次に計画道路予定線までセットバックした商業ビル（第4世代）への建替えが行われている。

　　つまりキャットストリートの無秩序さは、川が道にかわるのに合わせた用途地域指定や容積率、防火基準の変更を背景としてもっている。それぞれの建物は建設時の条件を形に定着することによって、都市空間の推移を時間的にも空間的にもランダムに提示している。こうしたゾーニングの変化と組み合せを追跡すると、現状の8分割を含めて1943年以降延べ47分割されてきたことがわかった。このゾーニングに時間的推移をかけ合わせた「時空間ゾーニング」こそコマージデンスに隠された秩序なのである。

Commersidence

"Commersidence" refers to a pattern in which the activity of a commercial zone overflows into an abutting residential district. The Shibuya River was designated for development as a road in the lead-up to the 1964 Tokyo Olympics and covered with a culvert. It was initially turned into a pedestrian mall which ran through a group of small houses (1st generation). Then the 80s, after second-hand clothing shops (2nd generation) began to spring up in renovated houses, the area came to be known as "Cat Street." In 1996, after the roads were widened, it finally became possible to build on the road-side lots, leading first to three-story, steel-framed shops (3rd generation), and then the reconstruction of commercial buildings (4th generation) set back on the edge of a proposed new road.

In other words, the visual disorder of Cat Street is rooted in regulatory changes that arose in the process of the river's transformation into a road. With forms determined by the conditions at the time that each era's buildings were built, the area displays random shifts in urban space in terms of both space and time. By tracing these changes and combinations in zoning, it becomes clear that the area can be divided into a total of 47 sections dating to 1943. Through this method of "time-space zoning," in which a temporal shift is added to a spatial shift, we can discover the order that is concealed within this commersidence.

Commercial (2006)   Residential (1951)

世代の異なる建物が混在するキャットストリートの街並
The Townscape of Cat Street with Its Combination of Buildings from Various Generations

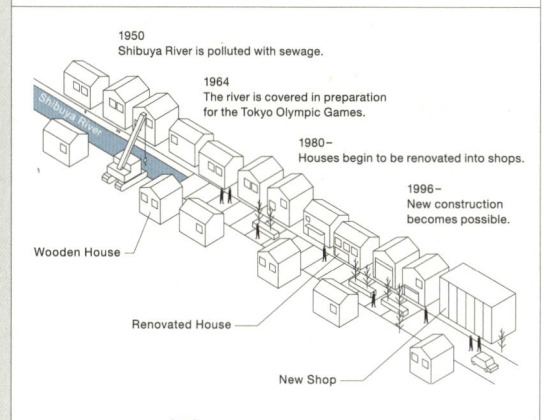

1950 Shibuya River is polluted with sewage.
1964 The river is covered in preparation for the Tokyo Olympic Games.
1980– Houses begin to be renovated into shops.
1996– New construction becomes possible.

Wooden House
Renovated House
New Shop

キャットストリートの変遷
The Transformation of Cat Street

1943 / 1996 / 1973 / 2007

キャットストリートを中心とした渋谷区神宮前における各年代のゾーニング
Era-by-Era Zoning Changes in the Jingu-mae, Shibuya Area Centering on Cat Street

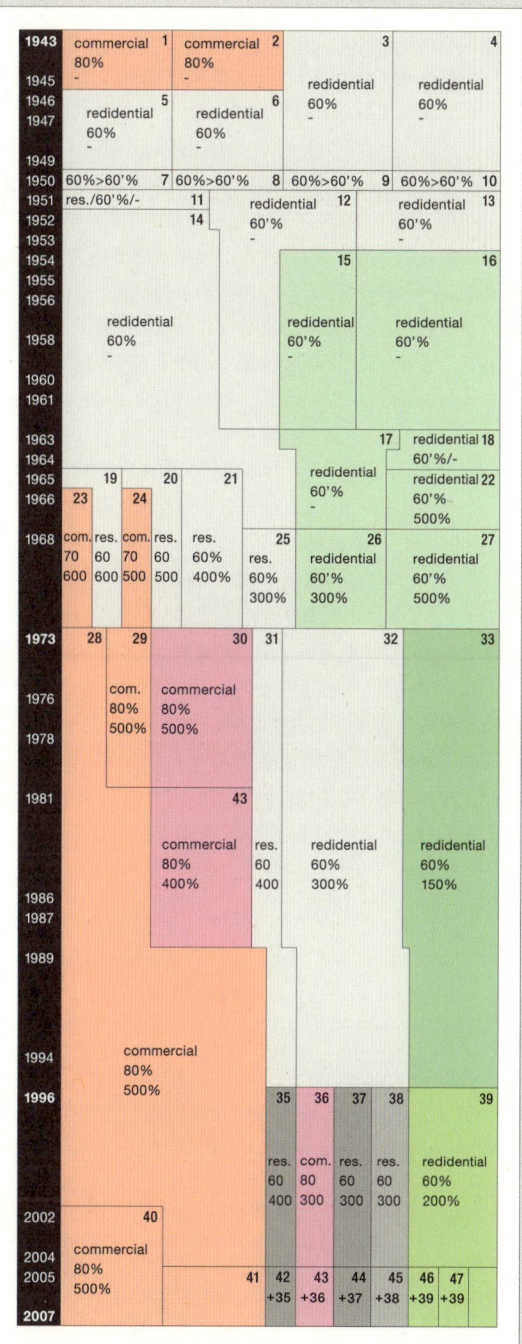

キャットストリートの時空間ゾーニング
Time-Space Zoning in Cat Street

サブディバーバン

　郊外住宅地（Suburban）が都市化の波に飲み込まれて細分化（subdivide）されることによって生まれるパタンがサブディバーバン（Subdivurban）である。東京駅から10km離れたところに位置する奥沢は、1920年代から始まった東京最初の郊外住宅地である。この地域は、昭和初期の「玉川全円耕地整理事業」や田園調布の開発など、開発当初から計画的な道路整備により生け垣の連続する良好な住居環境が整えられてきた。しかし近年では、土地を相続する際に起こる土地の分割やミニ開発による土地の細分化が行われることで、大きな地所が短冊状やクルドサック状、旗竿状へと分割され、生け垣が失われる現象がよく見られる。

　こうした土地の細分化は、不動産の路線価が高ければ高いほど、敷地が広ければ広いほど起こりやすい。それは世帯主の交替に伴い高い相続税が課せられるからである。かつては親の土地を兄弟が仲良く分割すればよかったのであるが、少子化が進むなか1人の子供では相続税が支払いきれない故に土地を細分化して売るなどの方策を取る必要にかられている。1940年からの宅地割図を年を追って見ていくと、この90年間で売りに出される宅地の面積は80坪から20坪強へと約3分の1に縮小していることがわかる。

Subdivurban

"Subdivurban" refers to patterns that emerge when a suburb is subdivided after being swallowed in a wave of urbanization. Okusawa, located about ten kilometers from Tokyo Station, was developed as Tokyo's first suburb in the 1920s. Like the Tamagawa Arable Land Administration Project and the development of Denenchofu in the early Showa Period, the area was designed to be a pleasant, shrubbery-lined residential area with systematic road maintenance. In recent years, however, as the plots have been subdivided after being inherited by successive generations and used for mini-development projects, large properties have been made into strips, cul-de-sacs, and flagpole lots, and the greenery has largely disappeared.

　The higher the tax assessment becomes, the more likely it is for a large property to be subdivided. This is due to the high inheritance tax that is imposed when the head of a household changes. While in the past, the children would cordially divide up their parents' land, with the increasingly low birth rate, an only child by necessity must resort to measures such as subdividing and selling the property. By chronologically examining the tendency to divide residential land since 1940 in the diagrams at right, one finds that the area of the lots sold over the last 90 years has shrunk to approximately one third the original size, or from 240 to 80 square meters.

多世代の住宅が混在する奥沢の街並 (2009)
The Townscape of Okusawa, with Its Mixture of Multigenerational Houses (2009)

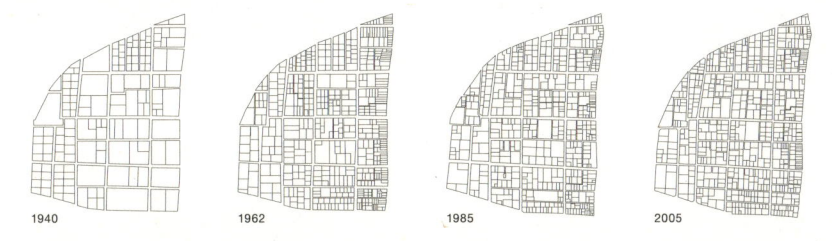

1940　1962　1985　2005

奥沢の各年代の宅地割図からみた土地の細分化の進行の状況。水平に高密度化する都市のモデル。(『ゼンリン住宅地図（世田谷区）』をもとに作成)
The increasing tendency to subdivide land can be seen in these diagrams of houses from each era in Okusawa. The increase in urban density is represented horizontally. (Based on *Zenrin Housing Map {Setagaya}*.)

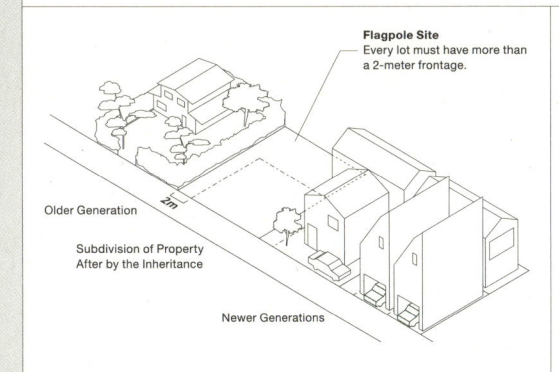

土地の細分化のされ方
分割された土地のどちらもが道路に2m以上面さなければならないという条件から、旗竿状の敷地などの土地の形態が発生する。
Methods of Subdividing Land
As conditions stipulate that each section of a divided lot must abut the street for a distance of no less than two meters, flagpole and other kinds of lots have become symbolic of this process.

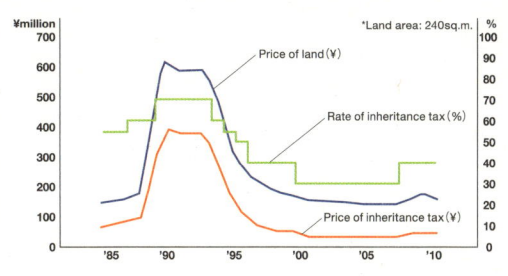

相続税額の推移
世田谷区奥沢4-16-12の公示価格の変遷をもとに、母無し子供1人で父親が死亡した場合の各時期の土地240m²の価格を算出し、そこから基礎控除を差し引いた課税遺産総額に応じた相続税率をかけて相続税額の合計を算出した(控除額は除く)。ここでは特に地価上昇が激しかった1980年以降の資料を示す。90年代前半、相続税は3億円を超え、これが敷地の細分化を後押しした。
Changes in Inheritance Tax Rates
Based on changes in land values in 4-16-12 Okusawa, Setagaya, we took the price of a 240-square-meter lot in each era and calculated the total amount of inheritance tax after subtracting standard deductions and multiplying the figure by the taxable-estate rate (excluding deductions) for an only child whose mother had already died and had inherited the land on the death of their father. The data clearly reflects the steep rise in land prices that occurred in the 1980s. By the early 90s, inheritance tax rates had topped ¥300 million, forcing more and more people to subdivide their lots.

次に戸建て住宅自体の空間の問題としては、住宅に世代があることを問題にしたい。短い周期で更新されながら戸建て住宅は確実に世代を刻んでおり、系譜学的にその変化を捉えることは、これからの住宅のあり方を考える上で避けられない。各世代の住宅は、それがその時代の人間が生きる条件になっているという強い認識もないまま、再生産され続けてきた。東京圏の場合、世代を分かつ具体的な特徴は以下のようになるだろう。

第1世代は敷地が80坪ぐらいあって、垣根に囲われた、ゆったりとした庭のなかに平屋の住宅が建てられる。車はまだないので垣根や板塀が連続し、家が庭木の向こうに見え隠れする街並をつくることができる。第2世代は敷地が40坪ぐらいになって建物が2階建てになり、自家用車の普及に伴い家の構えの一部が駐車場に割かれることになる。それでもまだ小さな庭は維持されている。第3世代はさらに敷地が細分化して25坪程度になって建物が3階建てになり、道路から引きをとる庭も確保できず、1階の間口の3分の2が駐車場によって削りとられるようになる。これら各世代がランダムに隣接するために、その街としての性格は全体の中での世代の配分によって決まる。逆に言えば、世代の配分を決めればその街並を類推することもできる。

もちろん今も住宅地の開発は続いているから、最新の住宅地にはその住宅地にとっての第1世代が建てられているのだが、先に述べた戸建て住宅の系譜から考えれば、2010年の今、新築住宅は、「第4世代の住宅」に歴史的に属することになる。そこに「第4世代の住宅で、なすべきことは何か?」という問いが浮上する。それを考えるのに、第3世代までの住宅を成立させてきた枠組みを反省的に再検討する必要がある。

隈研吾氏も指摘するように、アメリカ経由で輸入された持ち家政策は、バブル経済を生み出す都市経済原理を日本に持ち込んだ。土地の価値は上昇し続けるというまさにバブルを生む仕組みに従って、人間が生きる条件の具体化である住宅や住宅地は、上に述べた3世代の変化を刻んできた。この過程で戸建て住宅は、家族を経済活動の最小単位として自由に振る舞えるように、個別に囲い込んで共同体から切り離す装置としてプログラムされてきた。それぞれの家族が、個別に電化製品を買い、自動車を買い、服を買い、そういう一揃えを所有すれば、

3.
第1世代
The First Generation

4.
第2世代
The Second Generation

5.
第3世代
The Third Generation

Next, I'd like to examine the existence of multiple generations of houses in relation to the spatial problems of detached dwellings. In considering the state of these houses, it is essential that we understand the changes that have occurred with each generation of detached houses as they have been renovated over each short cycle. Houses from a variety of generations have continued to be reproduced without any special awareness of the necessary conditions for people's lives in each era. In the Tokyo area, these generations can roughly be divided into the following specific categories:

The first generation is represented by a single-story house built within a spacious garden that is surrounded by a hedge on a lot of about 240 square meters. As the structure predates the popularity of private car ownership, the hedge or wooden fence is continuous, and as the house is located beyond the greenery, it comes in and out of view. The second generation is exemplified by a two-story structure on an approximately 120-square-meter lot, one part of which, due to the introduction of private of cars, is allocated as a parking space. Despite this, some space has been maintained for a small garden. The third generation sees further segmentation, with a three-story structure occupying a 80-square-meter lot. No longer able to maintain a garden which is setback from the road, two-thirds of the first-floor frontage in this generation of houses is taken up by a parking space. As each generation abuts the next in a haphazard manner, and the character of the town is determined by the distribution of generations within the whole. On the other hand, by determining the distribution of generations, one can analogize the townscape.

Of course, residential districts continue to be developed, and even in these new areas, there are structures that represent the first generation, but in the lineage of detached houses, those built today belong historically to the fourth generation. This leads to the question of what should be done with this generation of houses? To properly address this, it is first necessary to reexamine the framework used to create the houses of the previous three generations.

As Kengo Kuma has pointed out, the policy of individual home ownership was imported from the U.S., and introduced to Japan as one of the urban economic principles that eventually led to the bubble economy. With the continuing rise in land prices that brought about the bubble came the aforementioned three generations of change in houses and residential districts, which embody human living conditions. In the process, detached houses allowed the family to act freely as a basic unit of economic activity, programmed as an apparatus partitioned off from each other, and isolated from the community. Each family bought separate electrical appliances, cars, and clothes, and the number of consumers increased simply by the need to individually purchase all of these things. A variety of areas benefitted as a result, including tax revenues, financial concerns, and social welfare programs, and both the family and the individual came to take on an increasingly fragmented role. This naturally exerted an influence on the form of houses, including the popularity of private rooms and other elements. Eventually things

6   1st Generation   2nd Generation   3rd Generation   2nd Generation   3rd Generation

6.
住宅の世代とその組み合わせによる類推的街並
An Analogical Townscape Created by Combinations of Multi-Generational Houses

それだけ消費者が増える事になるからだ。税制、金融、会社の福利厚生など様々な領域でこの装置は強化され、家族の、そして個人の粒子化は進行した。その影響は個室化などの住宅の形式にも当然及ぶ。そして住宅は家族のメンバー以外がいると不自然なくらいに、純粋に家族のための空間になってしまった。他者を招くことのない住宅は閉鎖的になり、空調機の普及もあいまって、軒先や庭のような、家のまわりの外部空間を極めて貧困にしてしまった。敷地の細分化と建蔽率の上乗せによって、敷地ギリギリまで建物の壁面が迫り、住宅建設は単なる隙間を副産物として生産するようになってしまった。こうした特徴からは、おしなべて住宅の空間を非寛容にする傾向を読み取ることができる。これらが相互に作用し合う非寛容のスパイラルに歯止めをかけ、人間が生きるためのもっと寛容な空間を、住宅を通してもたらすことはできないだろうか。

そのために第4世代の住宅が備えるべき3つの条件を掲げる。仕事場などを併せもつ事によって家族以外のメンバーがいてもおかしくなくすること、ロッジアを設けることによって半外部で暮らす機会を増やすこと、住宅建設の副産物である隙間を再定義することである。幸い資本主義が求める粒子化のテクノロジーは、携帯電話の普及で完成され、もはや住宅が負わなくてもよいのである。つまり第4世代の住宅は、個別化、粒子化のプログラムから解放されたのである。だからこれからは、むしろそのエネルギーを共同化、共有化へと反転させることができる。すなわち、限定された全体としての都市の中間単位との響き合いを通して個の建築の振る舞いを位置づけ、そこに混在する第1世代から第3世代までの戸建て住宅の系譜に対して第4世代の住宅を位置づけること、これによって20世紀の持ち家政策によって住宅が粒子化し非寛容になっていくプログラムを解除し、よりいきいきと暮らせる寛容な空間をつくり上げることが、東京が都市として卓越するために避けては通れない道なのである。

第4世代の住宅が非寛容のスパイラルから抜け出すための3つの条件

1. 家族以外のメンバーがいてもおかしくない

2. 家の外で暮らす機会がある

3. 隙間の再定義

reached the point where it seemed unnatural for anyone outside the family to be in the house, and the space became a purely domestic domain. The lack of invited guests led to closed houses and coupled with the spread of air-conditioning, exterior spaces around the houses, such as the eaves and the garden, decreased significantly. Due to an increase in subdivision and a more restrictive building-coverage code, the exterior walls of the structures began to push at the limits of the lot, and house construction became little more than a byproduct of these gaps. From these characteristics, one detects a trend toward overall intolerance in residential spaces. Isn't there a way of curtailing this interactive spiral of intolerance and creating tolerant spaces that are more conducive to living through the medium of housing?

In an attempt to achieve this, we have established three conditions that are necessary for fourth-generation houses: 1) bringing people from outside the family back inside the house; 2) increasing the opportunities to dwell outside the house; 3) redefining the gaps. Fortunately, with the diffusion of the cell phone, technologies of granulation, and the pressure of capitalism have been released from the house. In other words, fourth-generation houses have been liberated from this program of individuation and granulation. This makes it even more likely that we may be able to redirect the focus of residential architecture towards community and collectivity. In other words, by determining the behavior of each individual structure through the resonance that occurs between intermediate units and the city as a limited whole, and by establishing a fourth generation of houses in respect to the lineage of the previous three generations of detached houses that are combined within it, we find the potential to liberate houses from the programs of granulation and intolerance that came with the agenda of ownership in the 20th century and create tolerant spaces where people can live a more vital life in order for Tokyo to excel as a city.

The Three Conditions for Freeing Fourth-Generation Houses from the Spiral of Intolerance

1. Bringing people from outside the family back inside the house.

2. Increasing the opportunities to dwell outside the house.

3. Redefining the gaps.

Tokyo in Practice
Atelier Bow-Wow
Yoshiharu Tsukamoto+Momoyo Kaijima

アトリエ・ワンによる第4世代の住宅
Fourth-Generation Houses
by Atelier Bow-Wow

東京のいわゆる近代的な戸建て住宅という枠組みは、郊外住宅地が開発され始めた1923年に始まる。これに住宅の平均寿命の26年を単純に加算してみると、1949、1975、2001となる。つまり2000年以降につくられた住宅は、系譜的にはもはや第4世代と言える。アトリエ・ワンは1998年以来、東京圏に複数の住宅を設計してきたが、それは要するに第4世代の住宅を手がけてきたということである。これらの住宅はいくつかの条件を共有している。建主家族は30代、40代の夫婦。子供がいない場合も少なくない。職業はアーティスト、文筆業、編集者など知的でクリエイティブな仕事についており、家で仕事をする機会も多い。好奇心旺盛で、出来合いの住宅に飽きたらず、建築家の作品についても独自に研究をしている。そのため設計に関して非常に協力的であるが、特別に裕福というわけではない。敷地は新興住宅地ではなく、都心に近い住みこなされた住宅密集地にあり、20数坪と小さい。新たに取得される土地の代金に予算の大半をさかれ、建築費が圧迫を受けている。などなどである。こうした条件の複合した枠組みが、アトリエ・ワンが設計してきた第4世代住宅を生んでいるのである。この枠組みのなかで、前章で述べた戸建て住宅が「非寛容のスパイラル」から抜け出すための方策として、「家族以外のメンバーがいてもおかしくない」「家の外で暮らす機会がある」「隙間の再定義」の3つの条件があると考えている。以下、これまで実践してきた住宅作品を通して、住宅でできた東京の都市空間の性格と、第4世代住宅の建築言語としての傾向性を浮かび上がらせてみたい。

The so-called "modern," detached house in Tokyo dates to the development of the first suburb in 1923. By successively adding 26 years, the average life expectancy of a house in the city, one arrives at the first three generations: 1949, 1975, and 2001. In other words, houses built after 2000 should be seen as part of the fourth generation. Since 1998, Atelier Bow-Wow has designed numerous houses in the Tokyo area, and in effect, these have all been part of this fourth generation. There are several things the houses have in common: Their owners are married couples in their 30s and 40s, many don't have any children, are employed in creative fields (as artists, writers, editors, etc.) and often work at home. Filled with natural curiosity, though they may not have given up on readymade houses, they have studied the work of a variety of architects. This makes them very cooperative in the design process, but not overly affluent. The lots tend to be small (around 75 square meters) and located in crowded areas near the city center rather than a new residential area. Most of the couples' budgets have probably been spent on acquiring the lot, which severely limits the cost of construction. This composite framework serves as a rough portrait of the people living in a fourth-generation house designed by Atelier Bow-Wow. In order to help this generation escape the "spiral of intolerance" described in the previous chapter, we have arrived at the following three conditions: 1) bringing people from outside the family back inside the house; 2) increasing the opportunities to dwell outside the house; 3) redefining the gaps. As we reference to houses we have created, we would like to shed some light on certain characteristic urban spaces of Tokyo, made up primarily of houses, and certain tendencies as expressed in the architectural vocabulary of fourth-generation houses.

47

Tower Machiya

Sway House

House & Atelier Bow-Wow

Gae House

Ikushima Library

0 10 20   50m

Site Plans S=1:2800

ガエ・ハウス
Gae House

ガエ・ハウスは文筆家の建主の仕事場を備えた住宅として郊外住宅地の典型的な細分化の現象（サブディバーバン）のなかに建てられた。それまでこうした都市的背景は、住宅設計の文脈においては限られた敷地のなかで狭さを克服し、広がりを獲得するという実利的な問題として理解され、都市空間の問題としては検討されてこなかった。従って、都市空間の問題としてこの住宅を組み立てることが重要だと思われた。

この敷地で建てられるヴォリュームには、北側隣地と道路からの斜線制限がかかる。これにより削られる部分を水平に分節して屋根とする。屋根は壁より1mはみ出ても建蔽率に換算されないので、そのフットプリントはヴォリュームのそれより大きくできる。これによってできる、屋根の軒とヴォリュームの隙間をガラスで覆い、三方に水平な連窓を巡らした。白い金属板に覆われた外壁と隣家との隙間から這い上がった光は、スチールの屋根に反射して室内を穏やかに満たす。この家に行かないと会えない、まるでもう1人の住人のような光である。この窓との関係において、隣家との隙間は室内から眺めおろされる庭として、あるいは光をためるチャンバーとして再定義されている。

The owner of Gae House, a writer, asked us to design a house that was also equipped with a work space, in the typical subdivided, suburban context. Thus, we consider the creation of this house to be a significant step in learning to deal with urban space.

The volume of the lot is controlled by setback regulations regarding the adjacent property to the north and toward the road. The roof is shaped by following this controlled volume. As the roof can only extend up to one meter beyond the wall without violating the building-coverage code, its horizontal projection can be made larger than the volume enclosed by the wall. By covering the eaves, the resultant gaps between the roof and the volume, with glass, it is possible to line three sides of the dwelling with multiple, horizontal windows. The light that rises from the gap between the exterior wall, covered in white metal sheeting, and the neighboring house, reflects off the steel roof, gently filling the interior. As if the light too were a "resident" in the house, the light can't properly be seen without actually visiting it.

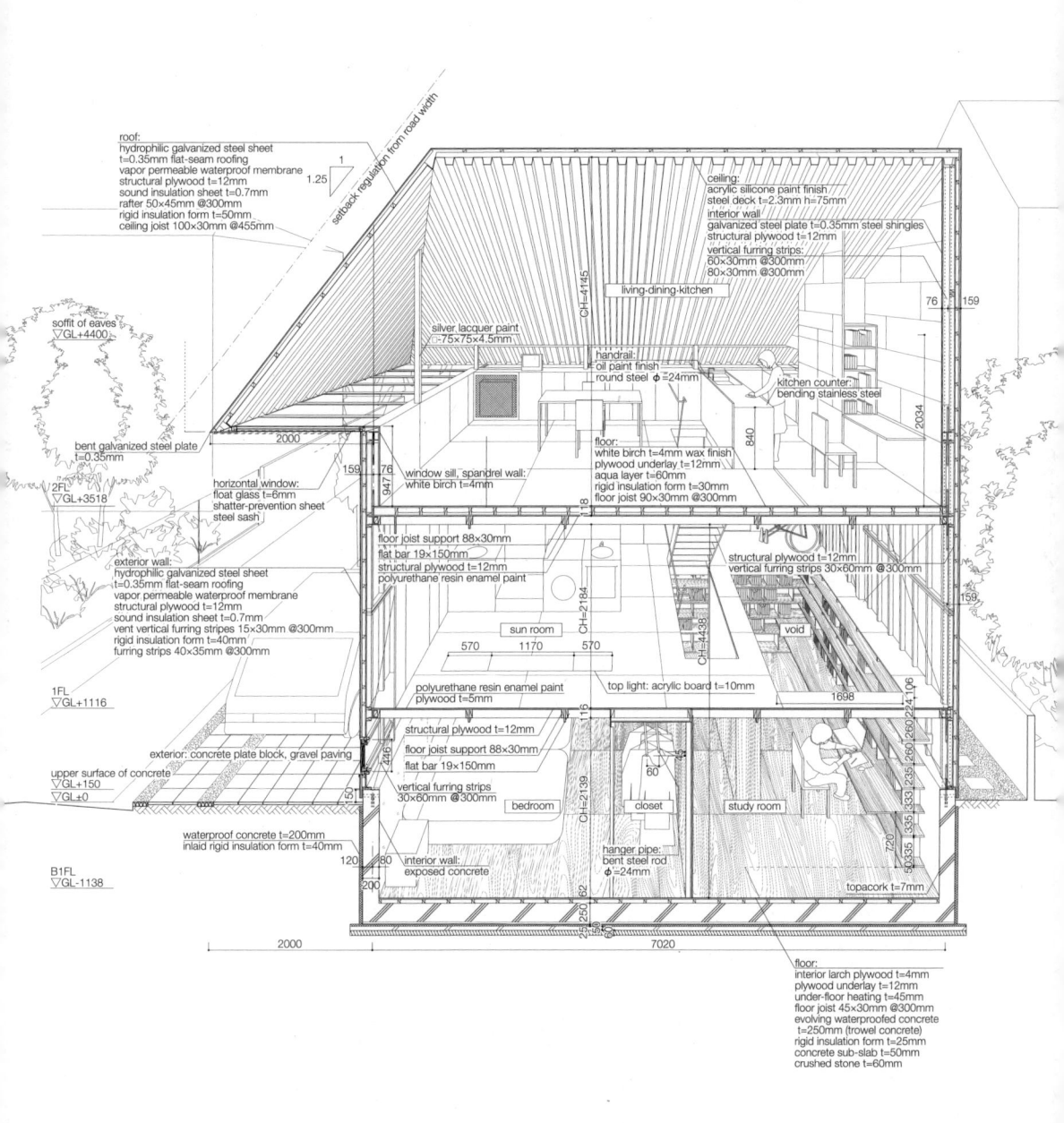

roof:
hydrophilic galvanized steel sheet
t=0.35mm flat-seam roofing
vapor permeable waterproof membrane
structural plywood t=12mm
sound insulation sheet t=0.7mm
rafter 50×45mm @300mm
rigid insulation form t=50mm
ceiling joist 100×30mm @455mm

ceiling:
acrylic silicone paint finish
steel deck t=2.3mm h=75mm
interior wall
galvanized steel plate t=0.35mm steel shingles
structural plywood t=12mm
vertical furring strips:
60×30mm @300mm
80×30mm @300mm

setback regulation from road width

living-dining-kitchen

silver lacquer paint
□-75×75×4.5mm

handrail:
oil paint finish
round steel φ=24mm

kitchen counter:
bending stainless steel

soffit of eaves
▽GL+4400

bent galvanized steel plate
t=0.35mm

2FL
▽GL+3518

horizontal window:
float glass t=6mm
shatter-prevention sheet
steel sash

window sill, spandrel wall:
white birch t=4mm

floor:
white birch t=4mm wax finish
plywood underlay t=12mm
aqua layer t=60mm
rigid insulation form t=30mm
floor joist 90×30mm @300mm

exterior wall:
hydrophilic galvanized steel sheet
t=0.35mm flat-seam roofing
vapor permeable waterproof membrane
structural plywood t=12mm
sound insulation sheet t=0.7mm
vent vertical furring stripes 15×30mm @300mm
rigid insulation form t=40mm
furring strips 40×35mm @300mm

floor joist support 88×30mm
flat bar 19×150mm
structural plywood t=12mm
polyurethane resin enamel paint

structural plywood t=12mm
vertical furring strips 30×60mm @300mm

sun room

void

1FL
▽GL+1116

exterior: concrete plate block, gravel paving

polyurethane resin enamel paint
plywood t=5mm

top light: acrylic board t=10mm

upper surface of concrete
▽GL+150
▽GL±0

structural plywood t=12mm
floor joist support 88×30mm
flat bar 19×150mm
vertical furring strips
30×60mm @300mm

bedroom

closet

study room

waterproof concrete t=200mm
inlaid rigid insulation form t=40mm

interior wall:
exposed concrete

hanger pipe:
bent steel rod
φ=24mm

topacork t=7mm

B1FL
▽GL−1138

floor:
interior larch plywood t=4mm
plywood underlay t=12mm
under-floor heating t=45mm
floor joist 45×30mm @300mm
evolving waterproofed concrete
t=250mm (trowel concrete)
rigid insulation form t=25mm
concrete sub-slab t=50mm
crushed stone t=60mm

Sectional Perspective S=1:75

スウェー・ハウス
Sway House

商店街化した神社の参道に沿って、小さな家が密集する住宅地に建てられたスウェー・ハウスは、イラストレーターの妻の仕事場を備えた住宅である。ここでは特に第3世代にはない外形ヴォリュームを、住宅地に出現させる可能性が探求された。その前提になったのが、2003年に施行が開始された天空率で、「地上の一定の位置において、各斜線制限により確保される採光・通風等と同程度以上の採光・通風等が確保されるもの」に対する斜線制限を緩和する新しいコードである。1階で接地する面積をできるだけ大きく確保し、これを最高高さ10mまで立ち上げるのだが、そのとき天空率をクリアするように空に接する面積を変えていく。最終的に、ボクサーがスウェーバックするように、ねじれながら地面から空まで一気に立ち上がるヴォリュームの振る舞いが見い出された。10mの高さを生かして、2つの異なる3層構成が螺旋階段で接続された内部は、斜め斜めへと下から上まで連続し、風呂のある屋上テラスへと到る。ガラス面での光の反射や、切り取られる風景の違いが、ねじれ壁にとられた開口のわずかな向きの違いを増幅している。

Located in an area packed with small houses along the approach to a shrine in a commercial district, Sway House is equipped with a work space for the wife, who is an illustrator. Here we explored the possibility of creating an exterior volume notably absent from most third-generation dwellings. This was predicated on the sky-exposure rate that was enacted in 2003 ("In a fixed position above ground, the amount of daylight and wind maintained under setback regulations shall be maintained at an equivalent or greater rate."), and a new relaxed policy regarding setback regulations. By maintaining as much ground space on the first floor as possible, the height was extended to an absolute maximum of ten meters to alter the area that is linked to the sky and satisfy the exposure rate. Ultimately, in the same way that a boxer adopts a sway-back posture, the volume, while curving, shoots straight up from the ground to the sky. By making the most of the ten-meter height, the interior, consisting of two different three-level structures linked by a spiral staircase, continues upward in a long diagonal line until it reaches the roof terrace where the bath is.

Sectional Perspective S=1:75

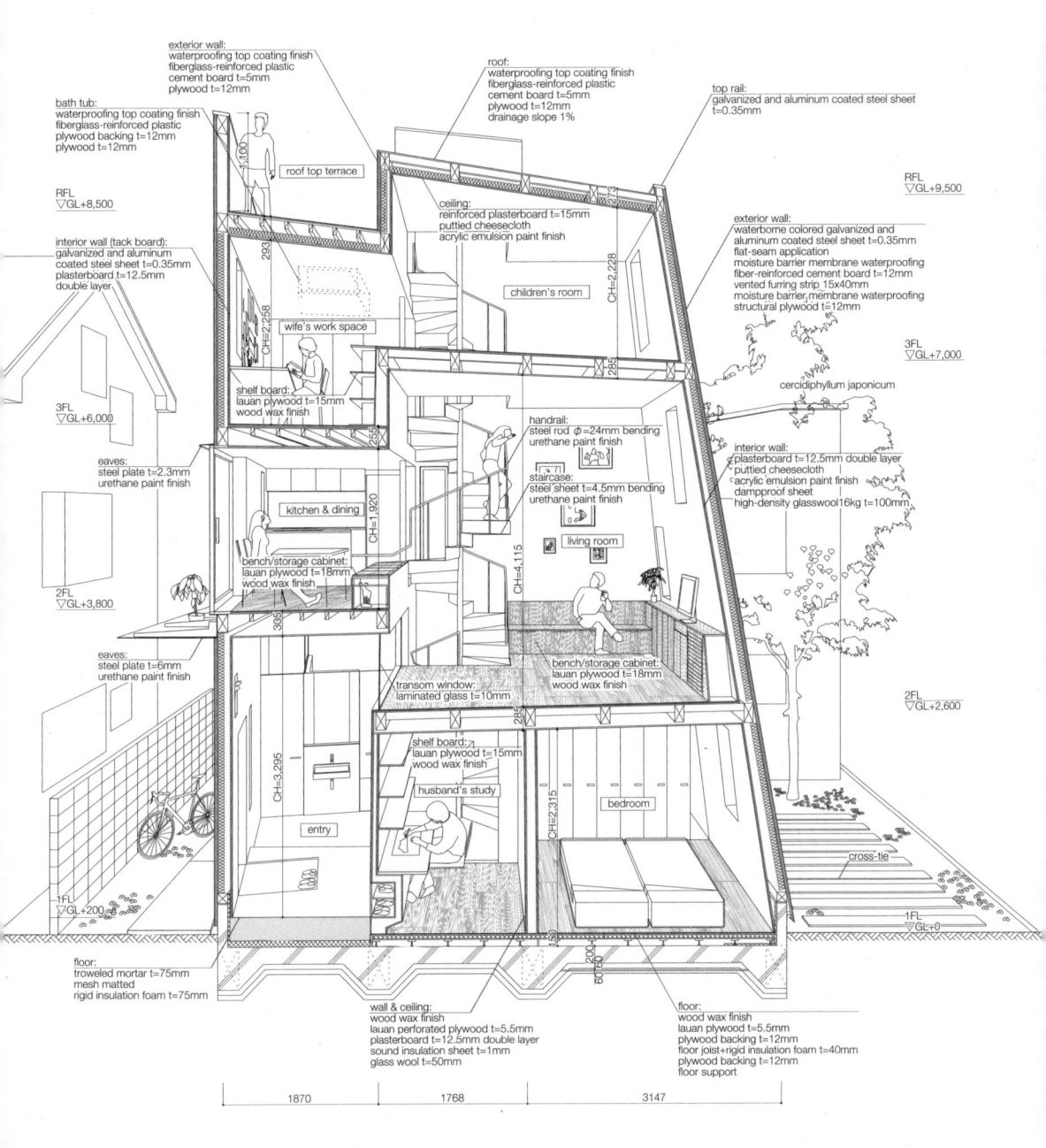

bath tub:
waterproofing top coating finish
fiberglass-reinforced plastic
plywood backing t=12mm
plywood t=12mm

exterior wall:
waterproofing top coating finish
fiberglass-reinforced plastic
cement board t=5mm
plywood t=12mm

roof:
waterproofing top coating finish
fiberglass-reinforced plastic
cement board t=5mm
plywood t=12mm
drainage slope 1%

top rail:
galvanized and aluminum coated steel sheet
t=0.35mm

interior wall (tack board):
galvanized and aluminum
coated steel sheet t=0.35mm
plasterboard t=12.5mm
double layer

ceiling:
reinforced plasterboard t=15mm
puttied cheesecloth
acrylic emulsion paint finish

exterior wall:
waterborne colored galvanized and
aluminum coated steel sheet t=0.35mm
flat-seam application
moisture barrier membrane waterproofing
fiber-reinforced cement board t=12mm
vented furring strip 15x40mm
moisture barrier membrane waterproofing
structural plywood t=12mm

roof top terrace

wife's work space

children's room

shelf board:
lauan plywood t=15mm
wood wax finish

eaves:
steel plate t=2.3mm
urethane paint finish

cercidiphyllum japonicum

interior wall:
plasterboard t=12.5mm double layer
puttied cheesecloth
acrylic emulsion paint finish
dampproof sheet
high-density glasswool 16kg t=100mm

kitchen & dining

handrail:
steel rod φ=24mm bending
urethane paint finish

staircase:
steel sheet t=4.5mm bending
urethane paint finish

bench/storage cabinet:
lauan plywood t=18mm
wood wax finish

living room

eaves:
steel plate t=6mm
urethane paint finish

transom window:
laminated glass t=10mm

bench/storage cabinet:
lauan plywood t=18mm
wood wax finish

entry

shelf board:
lauan plywood t=15mm
wood wax finish

husband's study

bedroom

cross-tie

floor:
troweled mortar t=75mm
mesh matted
rigid insulation foam t=75mm

wall & ceiling:
wood wax finish
lauan perforated plywood t=5.5mm
plasterboard t=12.5mm double layer
sound insulation sheet t=1mm
glass wool t=50mm

floor:
wood wax finish
lauan plywood t=5.5mm
plywood backing t=12mm
floor joist+rigid insulation foam t=40mm
plywood backing t=12mm
floor support

生島文庫
Ikushima Library

南北に深く東西に長い街区に旗竿敷地が多く含まれる住宅地の一画に、四方を隣家に塞がれた典型的な旗竿敷地を購入した夫婦は、2人とも家で仕事をする文筆家で、大量の書籍と資料以外に3人の子供を抱えていた。我々は当初、5人家族の家と考えて設計を進めたが、必ず本棚を組み込む段階でその小ささに窒息しそうになることに気づき、人と本の順を逆にすることを試みた。すなわちまず本のための空間を考えて、そこに人が住み込むという順に考えたのである。まず全体を壁が棚で覆われた本の家（2層）と、人の家（3層、半地下含む）に二分し、このずれを階段でつなぐ。本の家は仕事場兼玄関の1階で編集者に応客し、居間の2階で近所の子供たちに読み聞かせをする余裕がある。一方人の家は非常にコンパクトで、子供部屋などベッドと同じ大きさしかない。しかし人から本へと家の主体をずらした枠組みの変更によって、こうした小ささを家族は愉快なこととして受け入れてくれた。寄棟の屋根の下、それぞれ宝形の天井を持つ2つの家が平面的にずれて、敷地の竿部分に対応したへこみが生まれ開口を集める。通りからは本しか見えない本に捧げられた家。そこに人が居候している。だから家と呼ばずに文庫と呼ぶことにした。

This flagpole lot is located in an urban residential district containing many similarly-shaped lots. Both of the owners are writers and in addition to a large quantity of books and other documents, the couple has three children. We came up with a space for the books first and then imagined people living there. First, we divided the work into a house for the books with walls that were completely covered with shelves and a house for the people, and connected the gap of floor levels with a staircase. The book house was designed to host visiting editors in the work space-cum-entrance on the first floor, leaving enough space to read to neighborhood children in the second-floor living room. The people's house, however, became extremely compact, with some spaces, like the children's rooms, only as big as a bed. But by shifting the overall focus of the work from people to books, the family cheerfully accepted the small scale. Beneath a hipped roof, the two houses, with pyramidal ceilings, are staggered on the plane and the openings are collected in the indented section of the lot's pole shape. In this house dedicated to the printed word, books are the only thing visible from the street. The people here are only lodgers.

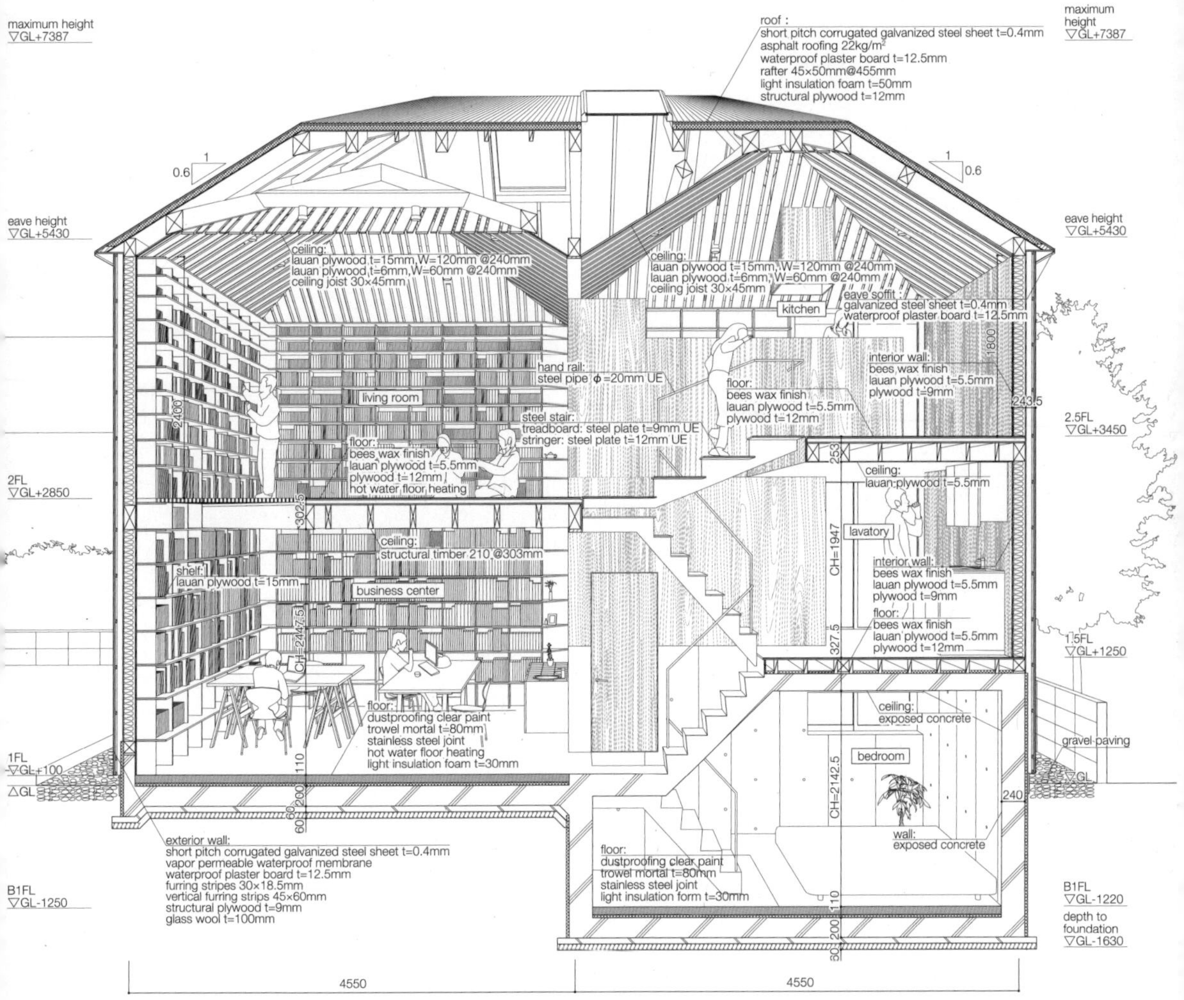
maximum height
▽GL+7387
roof :
short pitch corrugated galvanized steel sheet t=0.4mm
asphalt roofing 22kg/m²
waterproof plaster board t=12.5mm
rafter 45×50mm@455mm
light insulation foam t=50mm
structural plywood t=12mm
maximum height
▽GL+7387
1
0.6
1
0.6
eave height
▽GL+5430
eave height
▽GL+5430
ceiling:
lauan plywood t=15mm,W=120mm @240mm
lauan plywood t=6mm,W=60mm @240mm
ceiling joist 30×45mm
ceiling:
lauan plywood t=15mm, W=120mm @240mm
lauan plywood t=6mm, W=60mm @240mm
ceiling joist 30×45mm
kitchen
eave soffit :
galvanized steel sheet t=0.4mm
waterproof plaster board t=12.5mm
1800
hand rail:
steel pipe φ=20mm UE
interior wall:
bees wax finish
lauan plywood t=5.5mm
plywood t=9mm
living room
floor:
bees wax finish
lauan plywood t=5.5mm
plywood t=12mm
2435
2400
steel stair:
treadboard: steel plate t=9mm UE
stringer: steel plate t=12mm UE
2.5FL
▽GL+3450
floor:
bees wax finish
lauan plywood t=5.5mm
plywood t=12mm
hot water floor heating
253
ceiling:
lauan plywood t=5.5mm
2FL
▽GL+2850
302.5
ceiling:
structural timber 210 @303mm
lavatory
CH=1947
shelf:
lauan plywood t=15mm
business center
interior wall:
bees wax finish
lauan plywood t=5.5mm
plywood t=9mm
CH=2447.5
floor:
bees wax finish
lauan plywood t=5.5mm
plywood t=12mm
327.5
1.5FL
▽GL+1250
floor:
dustproofing clear paint
trowel mortal t=80mm
stainless steel joint
hot water floor heating
light insulation foam t=30mm
ceiling:
exposed concrete
gravel paving
1FL
▽GL+100
110
bedroom
△GL
▽GL
200
CH=2142.5
240
60
60
wall:
exposed concrete
exterior wall:
short pitch corrugated galvanized steel sheet t=0.4mm
vapor permeable waterproof membrane
waterproof plaster board t=12.5mm
furring stripes 30×18.5mm
vertical furring strips 45×60mm
structural plywood t=9mm
glass wool t=100mm
floor:
dustproofing clear paint
trowel mortal t=80mm
stainless steel joint
light insulation form t=30mm
B1FL
▽GL-1250
B1FL
▽GL-1220
depth to foundation
▽GL-1630
110
200
50
4550
4550

Sectional Perspective S=1:75

タワーまちや
Tower Machiya

車1台分しかない敷地に住宅をどうしても建てなければならない理由はない。しかし「床という床が全て畳の塔」などというイメージをそこに住もうとしている人から投げかけられたらどうだろう。しかも茶道に熱中する夫婦は、茶室を備えた家を望んでいて、行く末は師匠になることも夢見ている。非常に興味の湧く話を聞いて、我々はこの住宅を町家の系譜に位置付けることで設計を引き受けることにした。間口だけでなく奥行きも足らないので、上に伸びる塔状の町家である。最上階の道路側、つまり塔の一番「奥」に茶室が置かれる。そこに客を導く露地としての階段にまといつくように、畳、檜、モルタル、エキスパンドメタルなど、様々な仕上げの床が設置され、ふすま、格子戸、ガラスで軽く仕切られる。これらの断片的に浮遊する小さな居場所が、鉄骨の柱梁のリズムによって統合されている。立面にはあみだに組んだ華奢な鉄骨フレームが取り付き、わずか45cmの奥行きのなかに、格子戸やバルコニーが組み込まれることによって、町家であることと塔であることが統合されている。

There's no reason why anyone would try to design a house on a lot that only had enough space for a single car. But when faced with a proposal from someone who envisions living in a "tower in which all of the floors are *tatami*," what's an architect to do? Moreover, the couple, fervent practitioners of tea ceremony, also hoped to have a house equipped with a tearoom and dreamed of teaching there in the future. After hearing this extremely intriguing idea, we accepted the job by proposing that the house be something along the lines of a *machiya* (traditional wooden communal residence). As not only the frontage but the depth of the lot was severely limited, the *machiya* took the form of a tower that stretched upward. We placed the tearoom in the "depth" of the side of the top floor that faces the road. Then using the staircase as a garden inviting guests up to the room, The small living space that arose in fragments was integrated through a rhythmic arrangement of steel beams and columns. By installing a delicate, netted steel frame on the elevation and adding wooden louvers and balconies in the slight 45-centimeter depth, the *machiya* became one with the tower.

55

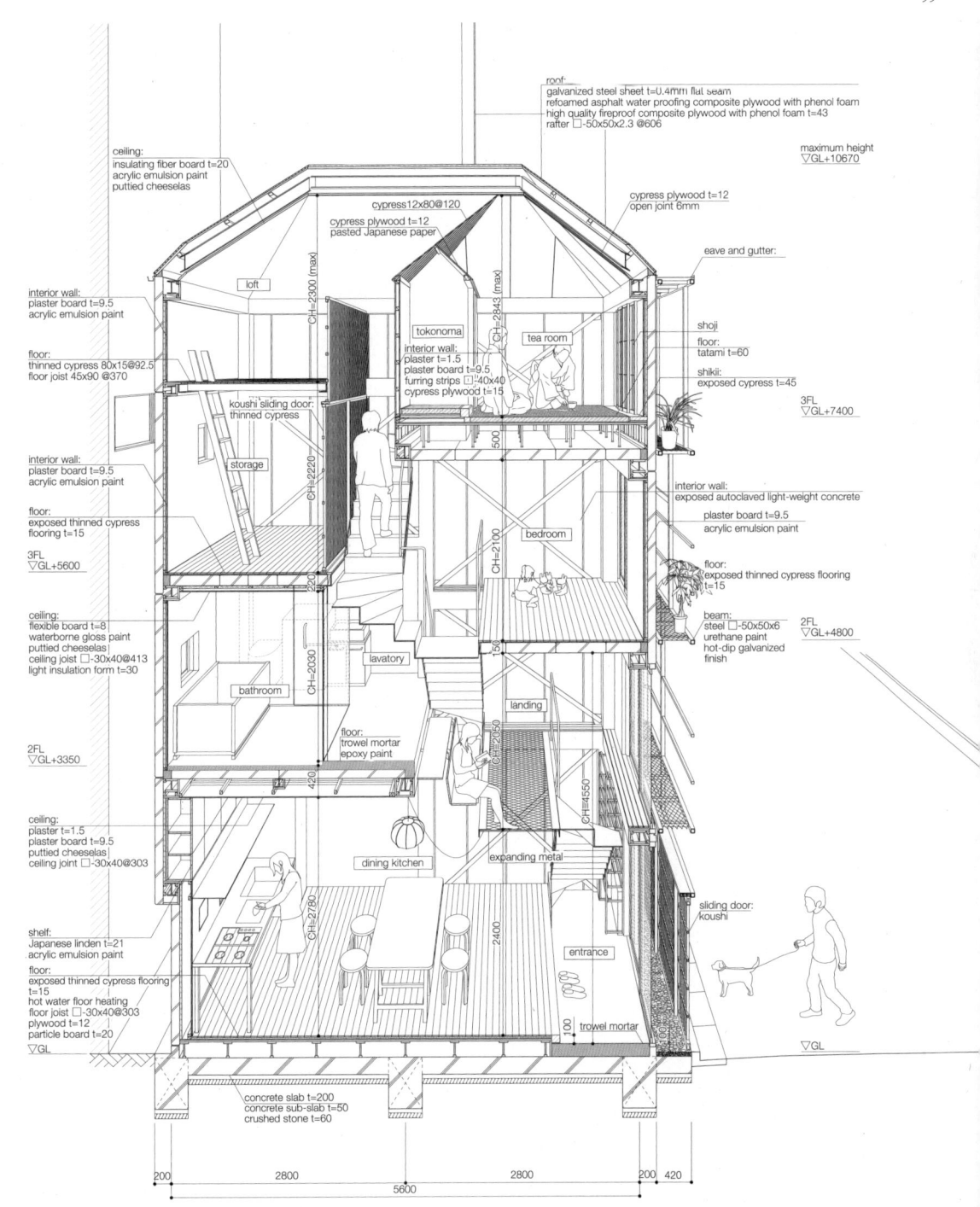

roof:
galvanized steel sheet t=0.4mm flat seam
refoamed asphalt water proofing composite plywood with phenol foam
high quality fireproof composite plywood with phenol foam t=43
rafter □-50x50x2.3 @606

maximum height
▽GL+10670

ceiling:
insulating fiber board t=20
acrylic emulsion paint
puttied cheeselas

cypress 12x80@120
cypress plywood t=12
pasted Japanese paper

cypress plywood t=12
open joint 6mm

eave and gutter:

loft

interior wall:
plaster board t=9.5
acrylic emulsion paint

floor:
thinned cypress 80x15@92.5
floor joist 45x90 @370

tokonoma

interior wall:
plaster t=1.5
plaster board t=9.5
furring strips □-40x40
cypress plywood t=15

tea room

shoji

floor:
tatami t=60

shikii:
exposed cypress t=45

3FL
▽GL+7400

koushi sliding door:
thinned cypress

storage

interior wall:
plaster board t=9.5
acrylic emulsion paint

floor:
exposed thinned cypress
flooring t=15

3FL
▽GL+5600

bedroom

interior wall:
exposed autoclaved light-weight concrete
plaster board t=9.5
acrylic emulsion paint

floor:
exposed thinned cypress flooring
t=15

ceiling:
flexible board t=8
waterborne gloss paint
puttied cheeselas
ceiling joist □-30x40@413
light insulation form t=30

lavatory

bathroom

beam:
steel □-50x50x6
urethane paint
hot-dip galvanized finish

2FL
▽GL+4800

2FL
▽GL+3350

ceiling:
plaster t=1.5
plaster board t=9.5
puttied cheeselas
ceiling joint □-30x40@303

floor:
trowel mortar
epoxy paint

landing

dining kitchen

expanding metal

entrance

shelf:
Japanese linden t=21
acrylic emulsion paint

sliding door:
koushi

floor:
exposed thinned cypress flooring
t=15
hot water floor heating
floor joist □-30x40@303
plywood t=12
particle board t=20

trowel mortar

▽GL

concrete slab t=200
concrete sub-slab t=50
crushed stone t=60

200 2800 2800 200 420
      5600

Sectional Perspective S=1:75

ハウス＆アトリエ・ワン
House & Atelier Bow-Wow

ハウス＆アトリエ・ワンはアーバンヴィレッジのなかの低層住宅が密集する領域に建つ仕事場兼住宅である。敷地はサブディバーバンに見られる細分化の結果である旗竿地であり、完全に隣家によって囲まれているために通りからその外形を伺い知ることはできない。こうした中間単位としての都市空間の性格に響き合う単体としての建築のあり方を模索することは、自分達がこの街に生きている条件をまずは直裁に物質化しつつ、それを個と個をつないでいく寛容な枠組みにつくり替えていくことである。そのつくり替えのための具体的な方策として、第3世代までの東京の戸建て住宅の系譜に対する批評に立脚した、第4世代住宅を構想する必要があるのである。

House & Atelier Bow-Wow is located in a crowded area of low-rise dwellings in an urban village. The flagpole lot is the product of subdivision, and as it is completely surrounded by adjacent houses, it is impossible to grasp the overall shape from the street. Seeking to better understand the state of architecture that is influenced by the character of an urban space as an intermediary unit, we set out to create an generous framework to link individual elements while directly cultivating the land as we ourselves lived in the neighborhood. As a concrete means of recreating the framework, we adopted a critical view of the first three generations of detached houses that were built in Tokyo and set about planning a fourth.

家族以外のメンバーがいてもおかしくない

1920年代に始まった戸建て住宅という系譜は、住宅は住居専用の地域に建設されるという都市計画的なゾーニングに従っている。すなわち、仕事をする地域と住む地域を分けるのが大前提なので、基本的には家族だけの空間へと純化されていく傾向をもってしまった。その結果、世代を経る毎に、家に人を招き入れるしつらいもなくなり、第3世代の住宅などでは家に家族以外のメンバーがいることが、極めて気を使う不快なことになってしまった。近代以前は商いや生産の場が家のなかにあり、使用人も多数出入りしていたし、書生や居候がいたことを考えると、現在の住宅の方向性は非寛容に向かっていると言えるであろう。この「非寛容のスパイラル」を反転させるには、まず家の空間に家族以外のメンバーがいてもおかしくない枠組みをつくるしかない。ハウス＆アトリエ・ワンでは、我々の住まいと、仕事場が1つの建物に納まるだけでなく、混ざり合うことによって、家族以外のメンバーが常に家のなかにいることが当たり前になっている。

Bringing People from Outside the Family Back Inside the House

The lineage of detached houses, dating to the 1920s, evolved in accordance with urban zoning measures that called for dwellings to built in special residential areas so the spaces of the houses tended to become simplified into family-only areas. As a result, with each successive generation, it became more and more difficult to invite people home, and the idea that anyone other than the family would be in the house had become a cause for discomfort. Prior to the modern era, shops and manufacturers had been located inside houses, and in comparison to the large number of users who went in and out of them, the contemporary house exhibits a strong sense of intorelance. The sole means of reversing this "spiral of intolerance" is to create an framework in which it is no longer strange to find people from outside the family inside a house. In *House & Atelier Bow-Wow*, not only are our living and working areas contained within a single structure, but a variety of people from outside our family are constantly visiting and mixing together inside the space in a natural manner.

水平に高密化する都市空間を支える
タテに連続する空間

住居だけでなく仕事場でもあるためには、何はともあれ大きさが必要である。そのためにヴォリュームを最大限確保するわけだが、そうすると建物の形はいわゆる家の形にはならず、高さ制限や斜線制限からある意味自動的に導き出されたものとなる。この場合は上に行く程2方向からすぼまって行くいびつな塊として現れることになった。これは都市が水平に高密化するなかで敷地が細分化されざるを得ない第4世代住宅にとっては宿命のようなものだが、このいびつさをいびつさにしない空間の枠組みを設定することが、デライトフルな振る舞いを生み出す上で欠かせない。ここでは、外壁が傾き始める高さ6mの線が、仕事の領域と住居の領域を分節する線として見い出され、その線に一致する2.5階の踊り場は完全に住居の領域で、小さな居間として使われているが、その線が階の途中にくる2階にはダイニングキッチンや大テーブルが置かれ、住居と事務所に共有される空間となっている。その下の1.5階の踊り場は模型置き場、1階は仕事場という具合に、最大ヴォリューム内部は様々なレベルに適宜確保された床で分節されている。これら大きさの違う床を、中央の列柱が部分的に傾きながらも結ぶことで、全体はひとつながりの空間として統合されている。

タテにつながる空間を熱環境の面から支援するのが輻射熱式冷暖房である。タテにつながる空間では、暖められた空気は上に、冷えた空気は下に集まるために、温風や冷風を吹き出す従来の空調機は向かない。下階と上階の温度差を縮めるために、輻射熱式冷暖房のラジエーターを各階に導入している。輻射熱は空気を暖めたり冷やしたりするのではなく、室内にある物の表面温度を一定に保つ。その熱源となるのが井戸により地下40mから汲み上げた、年間を通して摂氏15度の地下水である。これから熱交換してチラーのシステムを稼働させ、別の井戸で地下に戻す。夏には45日間も熱帯夜が連続して観測される東京都心で、これ以上冷房の排熱で都市を加熱しないように、この地熱利用のシステムが導入された。

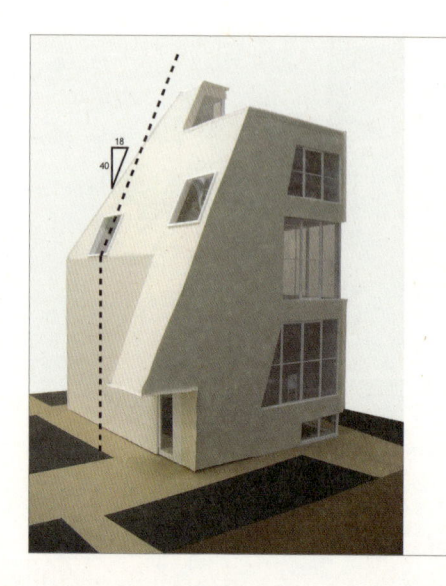

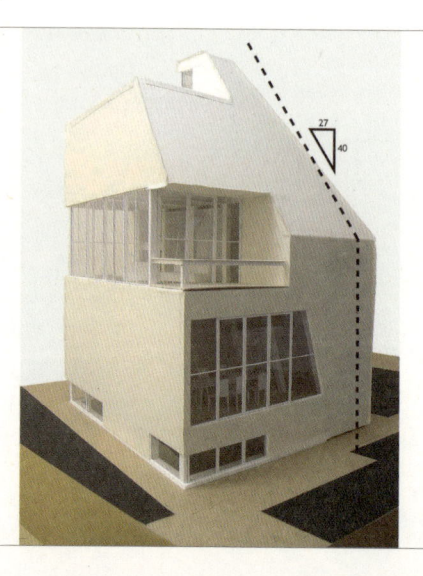

Continuous Vertical Spaces to Support Crowded Horizontal Urban Spaces

To create both a living place and a working place, a certain amount of space is necessary. We attempt to maintain a maximum volume, but in some cases, the shape of a house never emerges in the structure, which, in a sense, is automatically determined by certain height and setback regulations. The result is an awkward lump that grows progressively narrower on two sides as it rises. This can be seen as the fate of fourth-generation houses, products of subdivisions in a horizontally crowded city. Establishing a spatial framework in which the awkward aspects are ameliorated is essential in producing delightful behavior. Here, at the point where the exterior wall begins to slant, the six-meter-high line divides the working area from the living area. The landing on the 2.5 floor that links with the line completely partitions the living area and can be used as a small living room, but on the second floor, positioned in the middle of the line, there is a dining room/kitchen and a large table, creating a space that is both a living room and office. The landing on the 1.5 floor below is used to store models, and with a working space on the first floor, the interior, with a maximum volume, maintains a variety of levels and segments the floors. A central column, partially slanted, links these floors of varying sizes together and integrates the space into a single whole.

To support the thermal environment of vertically-linked spaces, we made use of radiation-style heating and cooling. As, in a vertically-linked space, hot air collects above and cold air below, traditional air-conditioners that blow warm or cool air are ineffective. To reduce the difference in temperature between the upper and lower floors, we installed a radiator on each level. Instead of heating or cooling the air, radiation heat maintains a fixed surface temperature of the objects in a room. The heat source for the system is underground water, which retains a constant temperature of 15 degrees centigrade throughout the year and is pumped from a well located 40 meters underground. After exchanging the heat and making use of a chiller system, the water is returned to another well. In the heart of Tokyo, where sweltering nights can sometimes continue for up to 45 days in a row in the summer, this type of geothermal system avoids creating any more heat through air-conditioning exhaust.

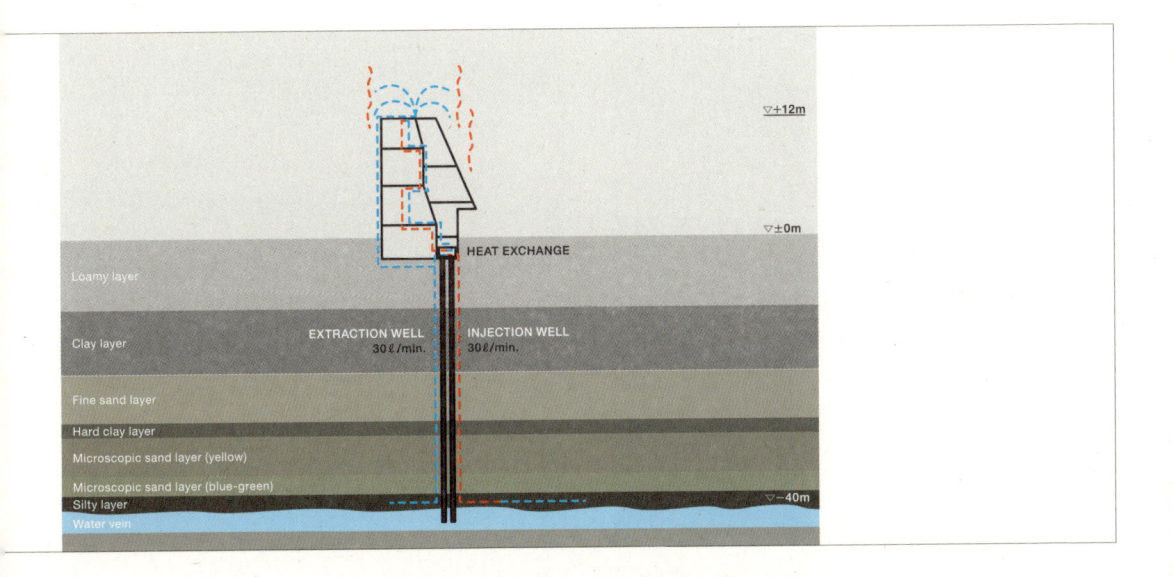

領有

タテに連続する空間に浮遊、もしくは宙づりにされた床は、壁で囲い込まれるかわりに、特定のモノが集められることによって特徴付けられ、他と区別されている。1階には靴、本、2階には模型、3階にはCDなどを集めた棚があり、極めて即物的に設定されていたにすぎない床に、収集されるモノを介した身体性による性格が色濃く投影されている。比喩的な言い方をすれば、それぞれの床が靴、本、模型、CDなどによって領有されることによって、それぞれに見合った人の振る舞いが召還されているのである。

Occupancy

Instead of having a floor that floats or is suspended in space vertically and completely surrounded by walls, one can add character and differentiate it from other areas by assembling special things. With shoes and books on the first floor, models on the second, and a collection of shelves for CDs and other items on the third, the floors are imbued with a unique character defined by the physicality of the objects, which are merely arranged in a practical manner. In metaphorical terms, by possessing shoes, books, models, and CDs, each floor summons up a corresponding human behavior.

家の外で暮らす機会がある

敷地の細分化は、庭を猫の額程に縮小し、住居と住居の距離を異常に近接させ、隙間に変えた。これが住宅の開口部のあり方に影響を与えないはずはない。一度隣家からの視線が気になると、窓が閉ざされカーテンが引かれ、外から家のなかは全く伺い知れなくなる。せっかくつくったバルコニーや庭も、内部との関わりを失っていきいきとした場所ではなくなってしまう。特にエアコンが一般化された第3世代以降、住居における振る舞いのほとんどは内部に閉じ込められ、おかげで住宅地を歩いても人の顔や姿は見えなくなってしまった。こうした非寛容な空間構造のまま超高齢化社会に突入するなら、独居老人の孤独死は今よりもっと増えるだろう。イタリアのロッジアや、オーストラリアのバルコニーのような、もっと家の外にいられる場所をつくっておかないと、人々のつながりという社会的な安全網を構築しようにも手がかりすらなくなってしまう。これをとにかく反転させるには、まずは家の一部であり外であるような空間的デバイスを用意するしかない。そのために、隣家との隙間に接したバルコニーや屋上庭園を設け、家の外側に振る舞いが表出する機会が多く用意されている。

Increasing the Opportunities to Dwell Outside the House

The subdivision of lots has greatly decreased the size of the garden, placed houses extremely close to each other, and changed the garden into a gap. Needless to say, this has also had an influence on the openings in houses. Occupants close windows, draw curtains, and generally make sure that the inside of their house is completely hidden from view. At that point, the desired relationship between the balcony, the garden, and the interior is destroyed and the house ceases to be a vital place. Starting with the third generation of houses in particular, due to the popularization of air-conditioning, almost all behaviors were shut inside, and as a result, even when walking through a residential neighborhood, it is extremely rare to catch sight of a person's face or form. If our super-aging society continues without altering these intolerant urban spaces, the number of solitary deaths among the elderly is sure to rise. Unless we create more places outside the house, like the loggia in Italy, we won't begin to be able to construct a social safety net to maintain links between people. To reverse this negative trend, the first thing we can do is make use of a spatial device like the outside section of the house. In order to do this, we should install balconies and rooftop gardens to connect the gaps with adjacent houses and create more opportunities to stay outside.

隙間の再定義

第3世代の住宅がひしめく細分化の進んだ住宅地であっても、建物と建物の間には約1mの隙間のような空間が残されている。これは隣家の承諾を得ずに建設するのなら、敷地境界から50cm以上外壁線を離すという民法上の数字が、まるで家づくりの基準であるかのように反復されているためである。敷地が十分大きければ庭になるはずの、敷地のなかの建物以外に残された場所、すなわちヴォイドは、敷地が小さくなるともはや庭になりえず、死んだ隙間になってしまう。家を建てることの副産物としてのヴォイドが、かならず隙間になってしまうことがわかっているならば、その存在を設計のはじめにフィードバックして、何か有意義なヴォイドにできないはずはない。

ハウス＆アトリエ・ワンでは、周囲の坂の下から連続する建物と建物に挟まれた隙間が、家のなかを貫通して、街の隙間に住み込んでいるようにした。具体的には、2階のリビングルームをできるだけこの隙間の領域へと拡張して考えた。そのために、2階は3面ガラス張りになっていて、そのうち1面は隣のアパートの壁面に対して全面的に開放されている。アパートの白い壁を、拡張された居間の壁紙として借りているのである。この「借壁」は、太陽の動きに合わせて微細な影を表面に落とし、表情を変える。旗竿敷地の竿部分も土地の細分化によって生まれる隙間である。が、ここでは特に日射条件の不均質さに注目して、多様な植物を植え、アプローチ庭としている。

Redefining the Gaps

Although third-generation houses are located in crowded and increasingly subdivided residential areas, an approximately one-meter gap has been maintained between the houses. Though construction might require the consent of one's neighbors, the civil code, which stipulates that the boundary of a lot must be at least 50 centimeters from the exterior wall, has been reiterated as if it was actually the standard for house-building. The places, or voids, that remain around the structure should allow enough space for a garden, providing that the lot is big enough, but the smaller a lot is, the more difficult it is to create a garden and as a result, the gaps simply die. If it's clear that there will be gaps, the voids that are a byproduct of building a house can be used as feedback at the outset of the design process and then turned into meaningful voids.

The narrow gap between houses that leads up from the bottom of the slope on which *House & Atelier Bow-Wow* is located was used to penetrate the center of the house and create a sense of actually living in this gap in the neighborhood. In concrete terms, we tried to expand the second-floor living room as much as possible to fit the size of the gap. To do this, we lined the second floor with glass on three sides, one of which is entirely open to the wall of the neighboring apartment building. The building's white wall functions as wallpaper in the expanded living room. And the expression of this "borrowed wall," bathed in subtle shadows that depend on the sun's movement, is constantly changing. The pole section of the flagpole lot is a gap, created by subdividing the land, that can be used for dwelling. Noting the particularly unequal distribution of sunlight in the space, we decided to plant a variety of greenery and create an approach garden.

第4世代住宅による空間的実践

歴史的に見れば、東京ほど建物の生産が個によっていながら巨大な都市空間がつくられたことはない。従って、そこから新しい建築が生まれてくる可能性が十分あるという意味で、東京は新しい建築のインキュベーターなのである。その文脈の上に登場する第4世代の住宅は、住宅でできた都市東京の、高密度な住宅地の環境を敵視して築かれる抵抗の砦ではない。建物だけで完結するのではなく、光や風や熱の振る舞いと有機的に結び付き、周辺環境の断片を引き寄せ、集め、互いに関係付けることによって、環世界のような1つの生態系を組み立てるものと言える。そうなることによって、1つ1つの住宅を、独立しながらも都市空間を横につなげていくものとして、プログラムし直すことができるのではないか。

東京では1粒1粒の住宅が更新されても、ヴォイドの存在は消えない。しかし、その性格はそれを定義している周囲の住宅のあり方によって有機的にも無機的にも変えられる。これまでの建築の歴史は、こうした現実のコンテクストに召還されることによって、換骨奪胎されて新しい建築の知性に生まれ変わるのである。そういう東京ならではの建築の知性が発現して、初めて東京が新しい建築の文化を生んだと言うことができるし、東京が都市として卓越したと言えるようになるのである。それが「ヴォイド・メタボリズム」の可能性の中心なのである。

Spatial Practice with Fourth-Generation Houses

In historical terms, there is no place with as much individual house production over such a huge urban space as Tokyo. As there is an ample amount of potential for new structures to emerge, Tokyo is truly an incubator for new architecture. The fourth-generation houses emerging in this context are not fortresses of resistance with a hostile attitude toward the crowded residential areas of the city. Instead of simply being enclosed structures, they create an organic link with the behavior of light, wind, and heat, and by drawing out, collecting, and forming a reciprocal relationship with fragments from the surrounding environment, engendering a single unified ecosystem. In this way, connecting each house with the urban space while ensuring its independence represents a viable means of reprogramming the city.

Even if each house, each grain, is renewed one at a time, the voids will not be eliminated from Tokyo. It is possible, however, to alter their character both organically and inorganically through the state of the surrounding houses that serve to define them. By summoning up a realistic context, it was possible in the past to adapt and engender a new form of architectural intelligence. By discovering this type of intelligence in Tokyo, it has become possible to create a new architectural culture for the first time, and thus, one can say that the city has excelled. This is the potential that lies at the heart of "void metabolism."

65

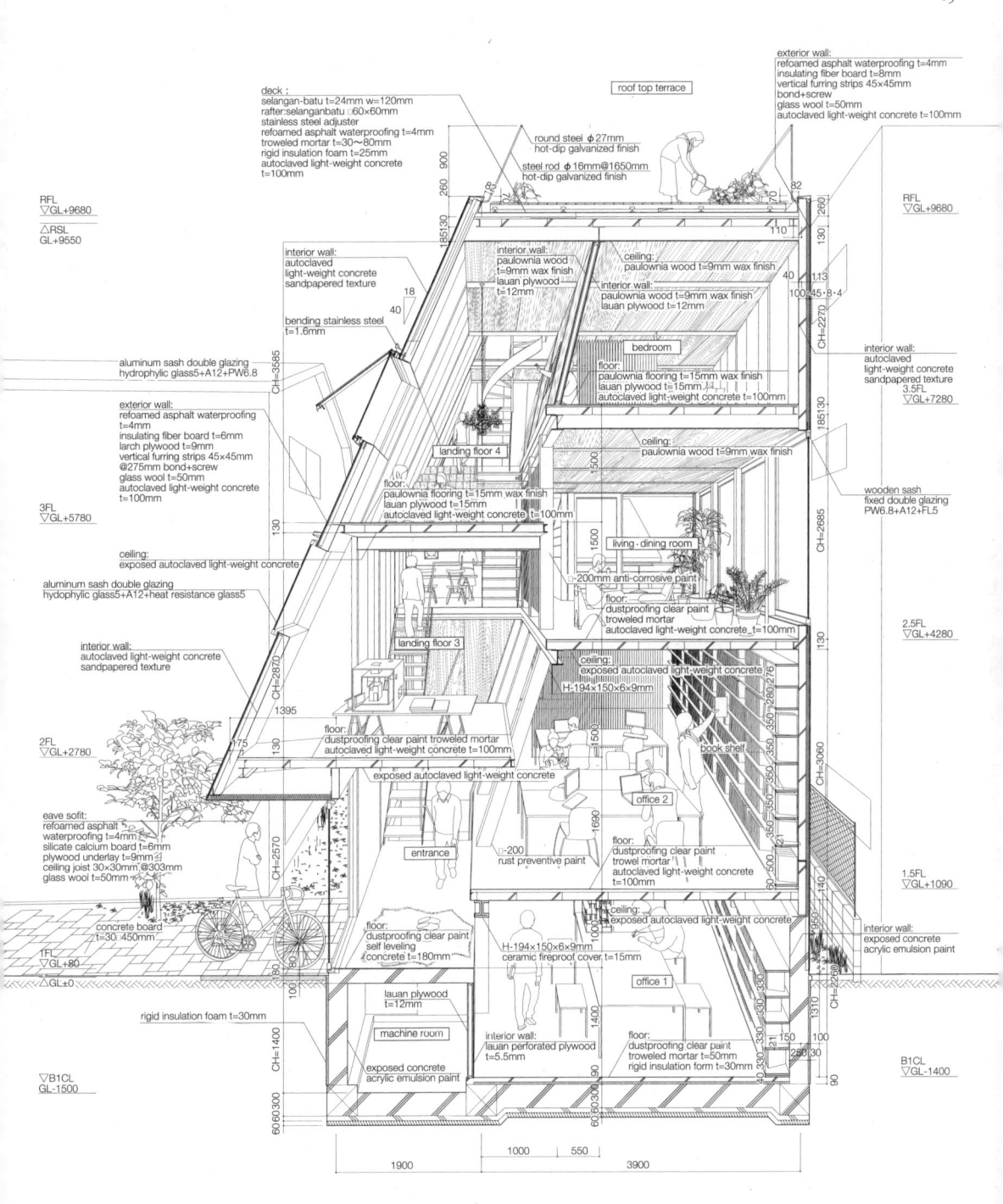

RFL ▽GL+9680
△RSL GL+9550

deck:
- selangan-batu t=24mm w=120mm
- rafter:selanganbatu □ 60×60mm
- stainless steel adjuster
- refoamed asphalt waterproofing t=4mm
- troweled mortar t=30~80mm
- rigid insulation foam t=25mm
- autoclaved light-weight concrete t=100mm

interior wall:
autoclaved light-weight concrete t=9mm wax finish sandpapered texture

bending stainless steel t=1.6mm

aluminum sash double glazing
hydrophylic glass5+A12+PW6.8

3FL ▽GL+5780

exterior wall:
- refoamed asphalt waterproofing t=4mm
- insulating fiber board t=6mm
- larch plywood t=9mm
- vertical furring strips 45×45mm @275mm bond+screw
- glass wool t=50mm
- autoclaved light-weight concrete t=100mm

ceiling:
exposed autoclaved light-weight concrete

aluminum sash double glazing
hydophylic glass5+A12+heat resistance glass5

interior wall:
autoclaved light-weight concrete sandpapered texture

2FL ▽GL+2780

eave sofit:
- refoamed asphalt waterproofing t=4mm
- silicate calcium board t=6mm
- plywood underlay t=9mm
- ceiling joist 30×30mm@303mm
- glass wool t=50mm

concrete board t=30 450mm

1FL ▽GL+80 ▽GL±0

rigid insulation foam t=30mm

▽B1CL GL-1500

roof top terrace

round steel φ 27mm hot-dip galvanized finish
steel rod φ 16mm@1650mm hot-dip galvanized finish

interior wall:
paulownia wood t=9mm wax finish
lauan plywood t=12mm

ceiling:
paulownia wood t=9mm wax finish

interior wall:
paulownia wood t=9mm wax finish
lauan plywood t=12mm

bedroom

floor:
paulownia flooring t=15mm wax finish
lauan plywood t=15mm
autoclaved light-weight concrete t=100mm

landing floor 4

floor:
paulownia flooring t=15mm wax finish
lauan plywood t=15mm
autoclaved light-weight concrete t=100mm

ceiling:
paulownia wood t=9mm wax finish

living · dining room

-200mm anti-corrosive paint

floor:
dustproofing clear paint
troweled mortar
autoclaved light-weight concrete t=100mm

ceiling:
exposed autoclaved light-weight concrete
H-194×150×6×9mm

landing floor 3

floor:
dustproofing clear paint troweled mortar
autoclaved light-weight concrete t=100mm

exposed autoclaved light-weight concrete

book shelf

office 2

entrance

-200 rust preventive paint

floor:
dustproofing clear paint
trowel mortar
autoclaved light-weight concrete t=100mm

ceiling:
exposed autoclaved light-weight concrete
H-194×150×6×9mm
ceramic fireproof cover t=15mm

floor:
dustproofing clear paint
self leveling concrete t=180mm

office 1

lauan plywood t=12mm

machine room

interior wall:
lauan perforated plywood t=5.5mm

exposed concrete acrylic emulsion paint

floor:
dustproofing clear paint
troweled mortar t=50mm
rigid insulation form t=30mm

exterior wall:
- refoamed asphalt waterproofing t=4mm
- insulating fiber board t=8mm
- vertical furring strips 45×45mm
- bond+screw
- glass wool t=50mm
- autoclaved light-weight concrete t=100mm

RFL ▽GL+9680

interior wall:
autoclaved light-weight concrete sandpapered texture

3.5FL ▽GL+7280

wooden sash
fixed double glazing
PW6.8+A12+FL5

2.5FL ▽GL+4280

1.5FL ▽GL+1090

interior wall:
exposed concrete
acrylic emulsion paint

B1CL ▽GL-1400

Sectional Perspective S=1:75

塚本由晴インタヴュー
聞き手：北山恒

街歩きで知った東京

北山 塚本さんも西沢さんも生まれ育ったのは東京の郊外だと思うんですが、その頃の郊外のイメージとか、東京の最初のイメージを話していただけますか。

塚本 僕は神奈川の茅ヶ崎で育ちました。東京から電車で1時間弱のところ。もともと半農半漁だったビーチタウンが別荘地化し、さらにベッドタウン化した場所です。でも、父は地元の会社に勤めていたので、ふだんの生活のなかで東京の風が入ってくる感じはなかったですね。

北山 1965年生まれというと、物心ついた頃は都市が拡張している最中ですね。郊外はどんどん変容していたと思うんですが。

塚本 僕が茅ヶ崎にいたのは15歳ぐらいまでで、そのあと少し内陸に引っ越しました。それが住宅地の拡大と一致していたと思います。要するに地方でも郊外は拡大していたわけです。

東京を意識するようになったのは高校生ぐらいで、1980年代の初めの頃でした。ファッションに興味があったので、広尾と恵比寿の間とか、恵比寿と代官山の間とかの古着の店を訪ね歩いていた。だから建築を少しかじり始めると、知っている建物が実は安藤忠雄設計とか、塔の家だったりして、それまでの街歩きが役に立ちました。

北山 塚本さんの学生時代はちょうどバブルのまっさかりだったと思いますが、どんな印象でした？

塚本 バブルの頃は、建築が雑につくられているという印象がありました。考えのない、目立てばいいという建物には全然共感できなかった。それで、大学の図書館にこもって昔の建築雑誌を見ていました。そこで1950年代の日本の建築のすがすがしさに出会いました。近代主義建築なんだけれどもコルビュジエやグロピウスやミースとは違って、どこか繊細で日本らしさが生きている印象がありましたね。

北山 それはどういう建築家？

塚本 広瀬鎌二さんとか、清家清さんとか、ケーススタディハウスの流れを汲んだものです。

卓越した都市

北山 塚本さんは学生時代にフランスに留学して、その後も世界のいろんな都市を体験されていると思いますが、そうした経験から東京という都市の特異性をどのように捉えていますか？

塚本 パリに1年あまり住んでみて、「パリは素晴らしい」と心から言えるようになりましたね。パリというのは卓越しているんですよ。いいとか悪いという問題じゃなくて、圧倒的なんですね。歴史的コンテクストに縛られて建築家に自由がないという批判はあまり意味がないと思いました。だから、東京も東京なりに卓越すれば、パリに劣等感を感じる必要はないと思って、パリから帰ってきましたね。

北山 東京がパリをめざす必要はなくて、オルタナティブとしての都市という概念があるということですか。

塚本 オルタナティブではなく別物です。住宅のような小さな粒を主成分に東京のような大都市ができていること自体、驚くべきことだと思うんですよ。土地が180万（個人170万、法人10万）の地権者に分有されていて、中国のように政治的に一気に変わることはありえないので都市計画は非常にやりにくいけど、それぞれの土地はそれぞれの人が管理し、家を建て、庭をつくりそのメンテナンスもやっている。街を歩いてみると意外に緑が多いけれど、その緑に税金が使われることはない。そう考えてみると意外にサステイナブルでしぶとい構造があって、部分ではフレキシブルに対応できる。人間が住む環境として悪くないんじゃないかなと思っています。

それに加えて、都市のコンテンツがものすごくた

An Interview with Yoshiharu Tsukamoto by Koh Kitayama

Getting to Know Tokyo by Walking Its Streets

Kitayama: I understand that both you and Ryue Nishizawa were born and raised in the suburbs of Tokyo, but can you tell me what kind of image you had about the suburbs at the time and what your first image of Tokyo was?

Tsukamoto: I grew up in Chigasaki in Kanagawa Prefecture. From there, it was a little less than an hour by train to Tokyo. Chigasaki was a beach town, which had originally been half-agricultural and half-fishing, that was first turned into a resort area and eventually became a bedroom town. But since my father was working at a company in the local area, I didn't really have any contact with Tokyo in my daily life.

Kitayama: Since you were born in 1965, I imagine that for as long as you can remember, the city has been in the process of expanding and the suburbs have been undergoing rapid change.

Tsukamoto: I lived in Chigasaki until I was about 15 and then moved a bit further inland. I think that happened at about the same time as the residential development boom. In other words, expansion was going on both in more regional areas and in the suburbs.

I first became conscious of Tokyo around the time I was in high school in the early 80s. I was interested in fashion, so I'd walk around looking for second-hand clothing shops between Hiroo and Ebisu or Ebisu and Daikanyama. Because of this, when I first started to get into architecture, the things I was familiar were Tadao Ando's buildings and the *Tower House* [designed by Takamitsu Azuma]. In other words, all of that wandering around the city finally came in handy.

Kitayama: You were probably in university at the height of the bubble economy, but what is your impression of that era?

Tsukamoto: I have the sense that during the bubble buildings were being knocked up all over the place. I had absolutely no feeling for things that were created simply to stand out and without any real thought behind them. So instead, I holed up in the university and read architecture magazines. That's where I first came across the refreshing Japanese architecture of the 1950s. It was modernist architecture, but somehow different from Le Corbusier, Gropius or Mies. It seemed more subtle and there was still something Japanese about it.

Kitayama: What architects are you referring to here?

Tsukamoto: People like Kenji Hirose, Kiyoshi Seike, and all the others who were involved in making case-study houses.

The Excellent City

Kitayama: You studied in France for a period during your university years, and I imagine you've visited a variety of cities around the world since then, but in light of all of these experiences, what do you think makes Tokyo unique as a city?

Tsukamoto: I lived in Paris for just over a year, and I can say from the bottom of my heart that it truly is an excellent city! I really think of Paris as the pre-eminent city. It goes beyond good or bad—the place is just so overwhelming. It made me realize that the common criticism that architects lack freedom because they are tied to historical context was completely meaningless. So by the time I came back to Japan, I felt like Tokyo could also excel as a city and that there was no reason to feel inferior to Paris.

Kitayama: By that do you mean that it's unnecessary for Tokyo to try and be like Paris, and that it can be an alternative city instead?

Tsukamoto: Not an alternative so much as something different. The fact that the chief component of a major city like Tokyo is a small grain like a house is amazing enough in itself. The land is shared by 1.8 million landowners (1.7 million individuals and

くさんある。たとえば登録されているレストランの数はパリが1万、ニューヨークが2万5千に対して、東京は10万で桁が違う。搾るとジュースがあふれ出るような都市だと思うんですね。やわらかな都市構造のなかにたっぷりうまみがしみ込んだような、ジューシーな都市空間になっているというのは、意外に高く評価できると思います。

街をダメにしない住宅

北山 僕が最初に塚本さんを知ったのはアニ・ハウスという小さな住宅です。普通の住宅とは全く違う配置計画を見せていて、小さな住宅つくることで都市全体のシステムまで波及するような感覚が面白いのですが、あのアイデアはどのように生まれたのですか。

塚本 たまたま、アニ・ハウスの敷地は、僕が子供の頃住んでいた町内なのです。兄が茅ヶ崎に戻って住みたいと、僕の親友の家の南側に敷地を買った。そこで、20年ぶりに行ってみたら、昔の茅ヶ崎とは違って、塀で囲まれた閉鎖的な家ばかりになっていた。

僕が子供のころの茅ヶ崎というのは、住宅と住宅の間にまだ畑が所々あって、畑にもなっていない空地では子供が毎日遊んでいました。住宅の外の空間というのはどこまでもつながっていて、それぞれの人がそれぞれに管理しているけれども、おおらかなもので、子供はどこでも自由に入って遊べる広がりをもっていました。つまり、非常に寛容な空間でした。だから20年後に訪れた茅ヶ崎はものすごく息苦しく感じました。そういう閉鎖的な住宅ばかりになったら、茅ヶ崎がダメになる。そのプロセスに荷担するのは残念なことだし、個人的にも許せないという感じがした。

同時に、閉鎖的な住宅はもっと極端な形で、日本の住宅建築の系譜をなしていた。その代表は安藤さんの住吉の長屋で、外側の都市に対してはっきりと閉じるわけ

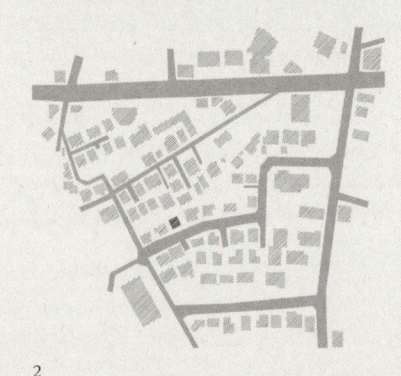

1.
アニ・ハウス
Ani House (1997)

2.
配置図
Site Plan
S=1:5000

100,000 corporate bodies), so a sudden political change of the kind we've seen in China, which makes urban planning extremely difficult, would be impossible, but each of these people oversees a plot of land, builds a house and creates a garden there, and takes care of its maintenance. When you walk around the city, there's a surprising amount of greenery, and it's not being maintained with tax money. When you think about it, the structure of the city is amazingly sustainable and strong, and in sections, is able to respond in a very flexible way. It's really not a bad environment for people to live in.

On top of that, there is a tremendous amount of content in the city. For example, the number of registered restaurants in Paris is 10,000, and in New York, the number is 25,000, but in Tokyo, there are 100,000—another order of magnitude. When you squeeze this city, juice is sure to come pouring out. A juicy urban space that is permeated with an ample amount of good flavor in a soft urban structure is something that works surprisingly well.

Houses That Don't Spoil the City

Kitayama: The first work of yours that I came across was a small residence called *Ani House*. It was interesting because the layout was completely different from a regular house and one had the sense that creating a small house had repercussions on the city as a whole. What inspired this design?

Tsukamoto: It just so happens that *Ani House* was built on a plot of land in the town that I lived in as a child. My older brother decided he wanted to move back to Chigasaki and bought a plot on the south side of my parents' house. Going back there for the first time in 20 years, I found that the town was filled with closed-off houses contained inside walls.

When I was a kid, Chigasaki still had fields here and there between the houses, and children played in the open spaces that hadn't yet been turned into fields. The spaces outside the houses were all connected and although each family took care of their own area, there was a sense of openness, and an expansiveness that made it possible for kids to play anywhere they wanted to. In other words, it was a very tolerant environment. But the Chigasaki I visited 20 years later seemed extremely stifling. The abundance of closed-off houses was ruining the town. I thought it would be a shame to contribute any further to this process and on a personal level, I couldn't allow this to happen.

At the same time, closed-off houses have a more extreme form and are part of the lineage of Japanese residential architecture. One example of this is Tadao Ando's *Row House in Sumiyoshi*, which shuts out the city, but Toyo Ito, Kazuo Shinohara, and Kazunari Sakamoto were also doing the same thing at that time. In residential architecture of the 70s, besides making a clear separation from the outside, the architects created attractive structures by enriching the interior. But I was left with the simple question, What would happen to the city if all of the buildings looked like that? Rather than making the city worse by building new things, isn't there some way of making it better?

In short, I began to think about how I might overturn the legacy of *Row House in Sumiyoshi*. If, for example, the building coverage was 50 percent, *Row House in Sumiyoshi* would be concentrated in the center 50 percent of the lot. So in addition to reducing the coverage of *Ani House* by ten percent, I squeezed the building into the middle of the lot and surrounded it with the remaining 60 percent of open space. Only one or 1.5 meters in width wouldn't have made any difference, but in order to set aside 2.5 or three meters, I came up with this kind of placement. Then, by also avoiding the use of a wall, your line of sight goes as far as the back of the lot and you can walk all

ですが、同時代の伊東豊雄さんも篠原一男さんも坂本一成さんも同じことをやっている。70年代の住宅建築というのは、はっきりと外と切った上で内部を豊かにするということで魅力的な建築をつくったけれども、そういう建築ばかりになったら都市はどうなってしまうのだろうか、という素朴な疑問がありました。建てれば建てるほど街がダメになるのではなくて、逆に建てれば建てるほど街がよくなるつくり方はないか……。

それで、端的に言うと住吉の長屋をひっくり返した。仮に建蔽率が50％だとしたら、住吉の長屋は空地の50％を真ん中に集めたわけですが、アニ・ハウスでは建蔽率を10％削って40％にした上で、建物をキュッと小さくして敷地の真ん中に建てて、60％の空地を外側にぐるりと回した。1mとか1.5m幅では他と変わらないから、2.5から3mぐらいはとれるようにしたら、ああいう配置になったんですね。さらに塀をなくして、敷地の奥まで視線が通るようにし、まわりを歩けるようにした。また、プランが小さくなってワンフロア・ワンルームになるので間仕切りがなくなり、四方向に窓があけられるようになったわけです。

変わる住宅のクライアント

北山 東京では塚本さんのような建築家に、自分の生活を支えるものとして、あるいは表現するものとして小さい住宅を依頼する人たちがいます。そうした新しいタイプのクライアントが東京には出現しつつあり、そこに新しい建築が生まれているのではないかという仮説を僕はもっているんですが、そういう感じはありますか。

塚本 そうですね。こんなに普通の人たちが住宅を建築家に頼んで、一緒に悩みながらつくり上げていくというのは、世界史的に見ても十分に卓越した住宅のあり方なのかもしれません。エジプトはピラミッドをつくったけれども、今の日本でピラミッドをつくっても意味がない（笑）。でも、住宅を集めて民主的につくられる都市は、エジプトではつくれないわけです。

クライアントとの打ち合わせは非常に面白いです。「今ここで家を建てて、こんな暮らしをしてみたいというのは、一体どういうことなのだろうか」と、住むということの文化的・社会的な枠組みにまで踏み込んで議論できる。想像力的にもジャンプがあります。

都市のもっているリズム

北山 東京というのは、かたい建築の形式や都市の形式がないから、ある種の自由が保障されている。枠組みそのものからイメージをつくるというところがありますね。東京という都市だからこそある可能性をどう考えますか。

塚本 1960年代のメタボリズムがめざしたのは、ライフラインとしてのコアと、個人空間としてのカプセルがあって、カプセルが何年か周期で更新していけば、持続性や拡張性のある都市がつくれるということでした。でも、2000年代の自分たちが今実際にやっていることは、隙間をあけた粒子化した都市のテクスチュアの1粒1粒を更新しているわけで、これはこれで都市の新陳代謝をしているという意味では、別な形のメタボリズムであろう。60年代のコアとカプセルに対して、隙間（ヴォイド）のまわりの粒（＝建築）による「ヴォイド・メタボリズム」なのです。東京が卓越するなら、この「ヴォイド・メタボリズム」の発展になるのではないか。

そのために住宅でやらないといけないことは大きく2つあると思います。まずは建築と都市の響き合いです。粒をまき散らしたような状態は均質のような感じがしますが、実際には断片的な都市形態が生まれつつある。都市全体と1つの粒としての建築はなかなか響き合えないけれども、「中間単位」ならば部分と全体の相互に影響し合う関係も想定できる。たとえば、いわゆる「カワ

around the outside of the house. In addition, because I made the plan smaller and created a one-room, one-floor building, there aren't partitions and you can open the windows on all four sides.

A Change in Housing Clients

Kitayama: In Tokyo, there are people who commission architects like yourself to create a small house in order to improve their lives or expressing something. I have a theory that as this new type of client emerges in the city, a new type of architecture will also emerge. Do you have the same feeling?

Tsukamoto: Yes, I think the tendency for regular people to hire an architect to build a house and deal with various problems together is probably one of the most ideal approaches to housing in the history of the world. In Egypt, they built the pyramids, but building pyramids in Japan today would be meaningless. [laughs] On the other hand, a democratically-made city assembled out of houses isn't something they could have created in Egypt.

Meeting directly with a client is very interesting. You can have a discussion with them that touches on the social and cultural framework of living and deals with questions like, "What does it really mean to build a house here and now, and to want to live this kind of life?" It also inspires imaginative leaps.

The Rhythm of the City

Kitayama: Since Tokyo doesn't have a hard architectural or urban form, there's a kind of guaranteed freedom here. I think that makes it possible to create an image based on the framework itself. What sort of potential does the city have by virtue of simply being Tokyo?

Tsukamoto: The Metabolist movement of the 1960s set out to create a city that was sustainable and expandable based on a core of lifelines and capsules of personal space that could be renewed after a cycle of a certain number of years. But what we're doing in the 2000s is renewing each grain of texture in the city, which has turned into a collection of grains with voids between them. In as much as this is also a way of metabolizing the city, you might say it's another kind of "metabolism." While the core and capsules were central to the 1960s, this is "void metabolism" based on the grains (or architecture) around an opening (void). If Tokyo is to excel, we believe it will be due to the development of this "void metabolism."

In order to do this, there are two important things that we have to do in housing. The first is to achieve a resonance between architecture and the city. It might seem as if scattering grains around would create a homogenous situation, but in fact, a fragmented urban form is emerging. It's not easy to create resonance between the entire city and a single grain of architecture, but with "intermediate units," one can envision a relationship in which the parts and the whole influence each other. For example, in a form that we often refer to as "skin and filling," there are "commersidences"—commercial activities that are mixed into a residential area (as seen in Cat Street)—and "subdivurbans"—old suburban residential areas that have been subdivided and include everything from first- to third-generation houses. My idea is that by picking out these intermediate units of urban forms in Tokyo, and understanding the behavior of the buildings as a whole within them, you can arrive at a continuous theory from the architecture to the city.

The second thing to take into account is the fact that the average life span of a Japanese house is 26 years. Because the cycle of urban metabolism is set at 26 years, shorter than the lifespan of a human being and shorter than the cycle in European cities, it has created the urban phenomenon of easily extractible

とアンコ」と呼ばれる形態、キャットストリートのように住宅地に商業が混ぜ込む「コマージデンス」、古い郊外住宅地が細分化され第一世代から第三世代までの住宅が混じり合う「サブディバーバン」。そういうものが東京のならではの都市形態の中間単位として取り出せて、そのなかでの群としての建物の振る舞いを捉えられれば、建築から都市まで連続した理論になると思っているんです。

　もう1つ注目しているのは、日本の住宅の平均寿命が26年ということ。都市の新陳代謝のサイクルが、26年という人間の寿命よりも短く設定されているがゆえに、ヨーロッパの都市に比べて短いサイクルで起こることまで都市現象として抽出されやすい土壌がある。1920年代に最初の郊外が誕生していますから、今我々がやっているのは第4世代になる。それは第3世代までの反省に基づいて組み立てられるべきだと思います。イギリスだと、住宅の寿命が100年。東京でいえば土木的なインフラストラクチャーのサイクル。そうすると、人間の一生のうちに建築もインフラも変わらない、要するに都市は変わらない。それに対して、ファッション的な商業施設はもともと短いサイクルで変わる。つまり、変わるものと変わらないものの二極で見られると思います。一方、東京というのは、インフラと商業の間に26年周期の住宅がはさまってしまったために、5年とか1年とかで変化する商業的な活動までもが都市の一部のような、空間の質を決めるものとみなされている。

　このように、「ヴォイド・メタボリズム」というコンセプトによって、変化する都市としての東京が卓越できるのではないでしょうか。

北山　生命体のようにただ動いているだけに見える東京というものが、ヴォイド・メタボリズムや中間単位という視点を与えることで、認識可能な都市として肯定的に扱える可能性がありそうですね。

塚本　そうですね。東京という都市がもっているリズムというか、時間的な尺度がカギになると思っているんですね。それは、社会学者のアンリ・ルフェーブルがリズム・アナリシス*で試みていた都市の見方とか、社会における空間の生産のされ方にもつながってくると思います。そうした時間尺度の問題というのは、20世紀にはなかなか触れられなかったんだけれども、21世紀になってようやく建築の問題として触れられるようになってきたのではないかと思うのです。

*『Rhythmanalysis』アンリ・ルフェーブル著、1992年

ground. The first suburb was created in the 1920s, so the ones we're working on now represent the fourth generation. Which means that we should be building them based on what we've learned from the previous three generations. In England, the lifespan of a house is 100 years. In Tokyo terms, that would be equivalent to the cycle of infrastructure engineering. Which means that in England, the architecture and the infrastructure don't change within a person's lifetime, and therefore, the city doesn't change either. By comparison, commercial fashion outlets change according to a much faster cycle. In other words, we can look at things in terms of two opposite poles: things that change and things that don't. On the other hand, in the case of Tokyo, because the housing cycle of 26 years lies somewhere between those of commercial facilities and the infrastructure, you can consider commercial activity, which changes every year or every five years, as the thing that determines the quality of a space.

In this way, based on the concept of "void metabolism," I believe it will be possible for Tokyo to excel as a changing city.

Kitayama: To recap, the application of concepts such as "void metabolism" and "intermediate units" holds great potential for Tokyo, which merely seems to function like a living organism, as a way of actively dealing with the city.

Tsukamoto: Yes, I think the key is the rhythm or the time scale of the city. This is also related to the sociologist Henri Lefebvre's view of the city as seen in his experiments with "rhythmanalysis,"* and the manner in which spaces are produced in a society. Time scale is an issue that wasn't dealt with much in the 20th century, but I believe that in the 21st century, it will ultimately be seen as an architectural issue.

Rhythmanalysis, by Henri Lefebvre, was published after the author's death in 1992.

Tokyo in Practice
Ryue Nishizawa

Moriyama House
7つの新建築要素
Seven New Architectural Elements

森山邸を設計している際に、僕らが問題にしていたこと、建築的・空間的アイデアのいくつかについて、ここでまとめて述べてみようと思う。それは主に7つくらいにまとめられる。すなわち、1. バラバラにする 2. 非中心性 3. 小さい 4. 環境をつくる 5. 透明性 6. 雑居・密集 7. 境界がない である。他にもあるかもしれないが今回はとりあえずこの7つについて。これらはどれも、森山邸の設計の前後またはその最中に、徐々に課題として現れてきたものであり、森山邸の設計を通して発展させたいと思った、建築的原理のようなものである。

I'd like to explain some of the architectural and spatial issues we encountered in designing *Moriyama House*. These can be broken down into seven main elements: 1) dismantling; 2) acentricity; 3) smallness; 4) the creation of an environment; 5) transparency; 6) multiple tenancy/density; and 7) the absence of borders. There may well be other concerns, but for the purposes of this discussion, I'd like to focus on these points. All of these issues are architectural principles which gradually arose before, during, and after the designing of *Moriyama House*, and were elements that I set out to develop through the creation of this work.

77

森山邸周辺の街に注目してみると、似たような大きさの木造建築物が密集して並ぶという風景が、まず目に入る。また、もともと田畑であったことから、通りが農地のような微妙なランダムさでもって縦横に並び、ランダムかつグリッドといえるような不思議な街路パターンになっている。その路地や通りは、地元の人々の生活感を感じる、魅力的な空間である。こういった環境の状態、都市構造というものから、森山邸の空間構成は導き出された。バラバラになっていたり、たいへん密集した状態であったり、屋内（家）と屋外（庭・路地）の反復であったり、開放性であったり、それらはどれも、建築スタディで出てきた建築的アイデアともいえるし、環境から受けた影響、ともいえる。

In examining the neighborhood in which *Moriyama House* is located, the first thing that becomes apparent is that the landscape is crowded with many wooden structures of approximately the same size. In addition, as the area was originally arable land, the roads crisscross in a vaguely haphazard way to produce a strange pattern that is neither entirely random nor gridlike. The alleys and roads are attractive spaces that convey a sense of the local residents' lifestyles. These environmental conditions and urban structure inspired the spatial composition of *Moriyama House*. Dismantling, overcrowding, repetition of internal (house) and external (garden, alley) spaces, and a sense of openness can all be seen as architectural ideas that emerged in our studies and were influenced by the environment.

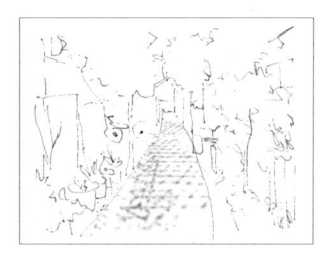

敷地周辺の路地には植木や木々がたくさん置かれていて、路地を自分のものであるかのように使っている。
In the alleys surrounding the lot, there were many plants and trees that could be used like one's own property.

舗装されていない砂利みちや公園などがあちこちにある。
Unpaved, gravel roads and parks can be found throughout the neighborhood.

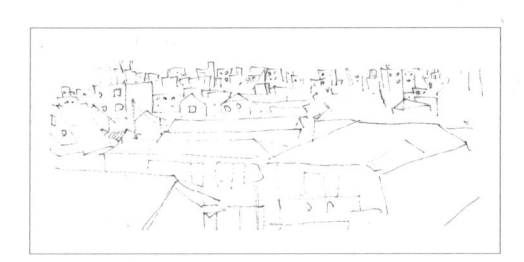

1. バラバラにする

「バラバラ」というのは、このプロジェクトではもっとも重要なキャラクターの1つである。もともと要求条件は、賃貸住宅とオーナー住宅で、それは本当は建築単体として応えるほうが東京では一般的であるような要求条件だったが、ここではすべてのプログラムをバラバラにして、各々離して配置した。

1. Dismantling

"Dismantling" is one of the most important characteristics of this project. One of the original requirements was the creation of a rental dwelling and a house for the owner, which in Tokyo would usually be satisfied by creating separate architectural units. But here, we decided to dismantle the program and distribute each of them separately.

バラバラにすることで、周辺環境との連続性が生まれ、風通しがよくなり、また、透明性が生まれる。バラバラにすると、当たり前だが建築は単体でなくなって、「群れ」の状態になる。そうなると、全体の関係性が見えてくる。関係性が、単にプログラムの問題にとどまらず、外観の問題にもなり、景観の問題にもなる。

Dismantling them established a continuity with the surrounding environment, improved the flow of air, and created transparency. And obviously, by dismantling them, the structure is no longer a unit, but takes on the character of a cluster. In this manner, it becomes possible to see the relationship between the whole. The relationship is not merely connected to the problem of programming but also that of the external appearance and the landscape.

森山さんのキッチン
The owner's kitchen.

E

3m×3m のへやが3層積まれたいえ
The house consists of three stories
of rooms with the same dimensions
(3m×3m).

A

B

C

森山さんは A〜D の4つのいえをもつ
The owner owns four houses (A–D).

森山さんのはなれ
いろいろな棟のひとがここに集まる
The owner's detached room.
People from the various wings of the house
assemble here.

D

I

森山さんのバスルーム
The owner's bathroom.

天井高が 4m もある大きないえ
The large house has a ceiling height
of four meters.

F

G

大きな 3 階建てのいえ
The large, three-story house.

H

小さなバスルームとガラス廊下で
つながっている半地下のいえ
The semi-underground house is linked
by a glass corridor to a small bathroom.

J

平屋の小さなワンルームのいえ
This small, one-floor structure is
a one-room house.

2. 非中心性

非中心性というものは、現代的な構造である。非中心性というものは、どこも中心になりうるような状態でもある。どこにいても自分が中心であるように感じる、非中心性のような多中心性のような、両方の状態といえばいいだろうか。端っこに住んでいても、自分の周りに豊かな環境が広がっているような、環境に包まれて暮らしているような、住み手がそういう気持ちになる、そのような構造をもった住居を目指した。

2. Acentricity

Acentricity is a contemporary structure. It allows any place to become the center. One might say that this creates both a sense of always being at the center and a sense of multicentricity. Our goal was to create a dwelling with structures in which even if the resident lived on the edge of the lot, they would be aware of the rich environment around them and feel as if they were encompassed in it.

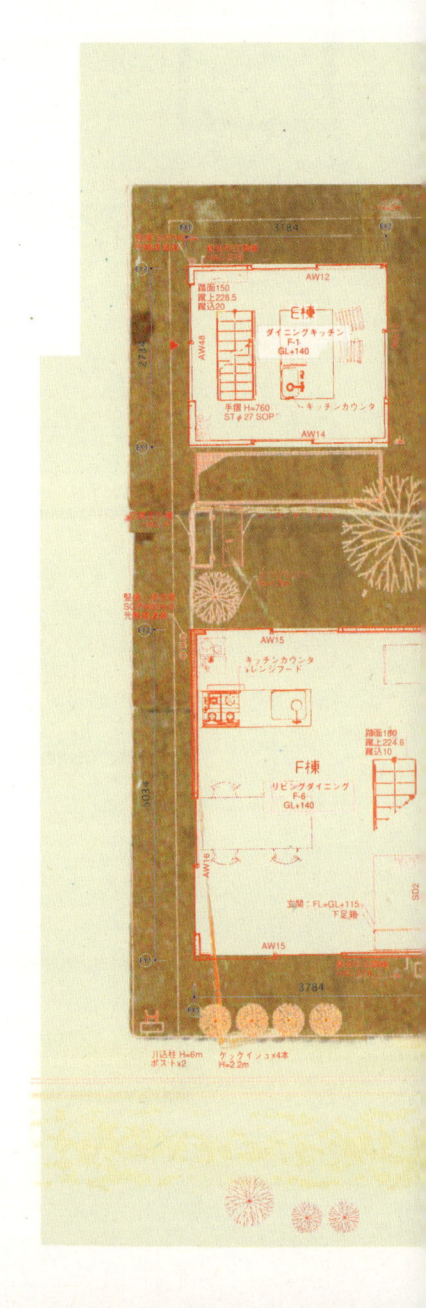

83

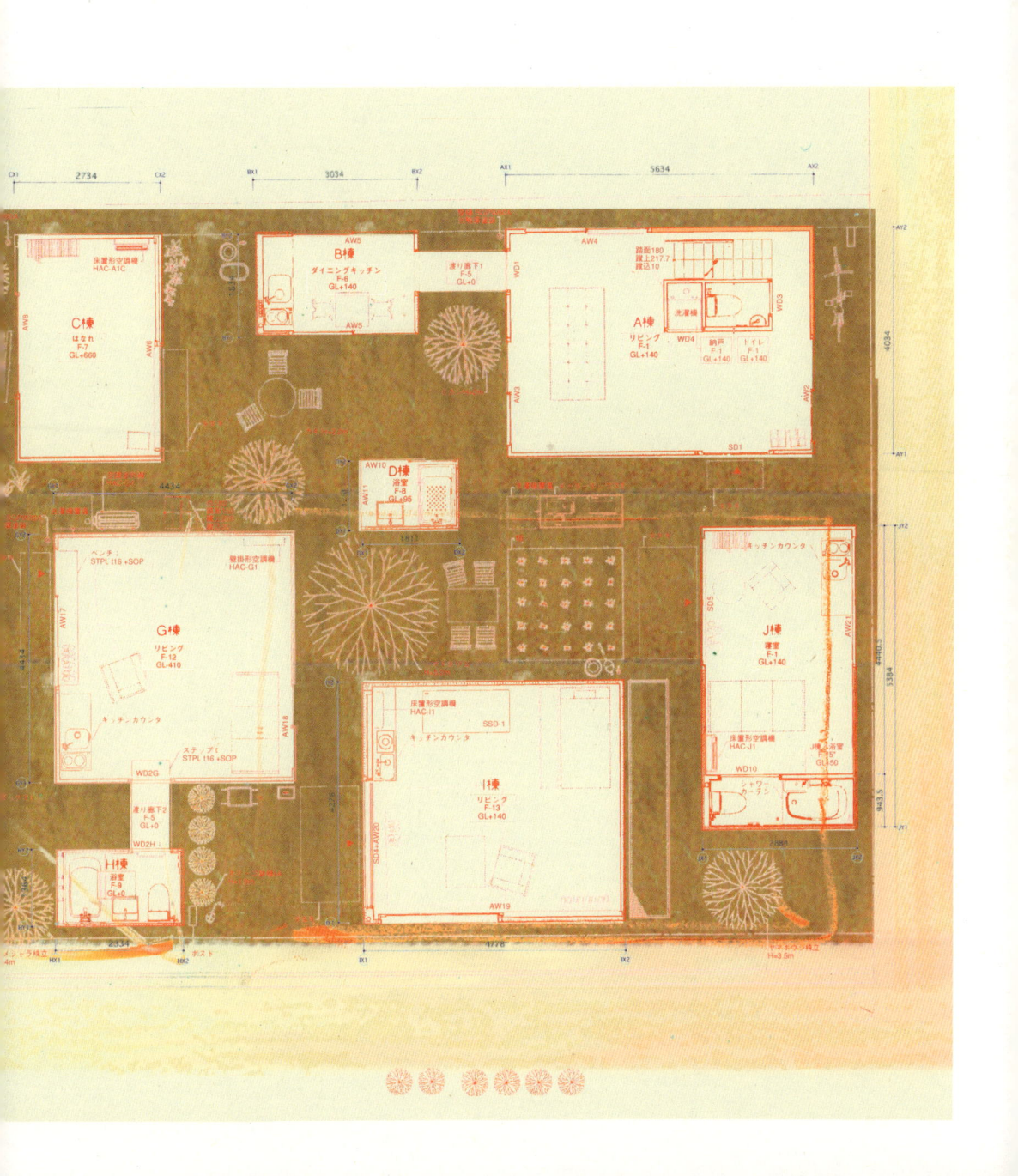

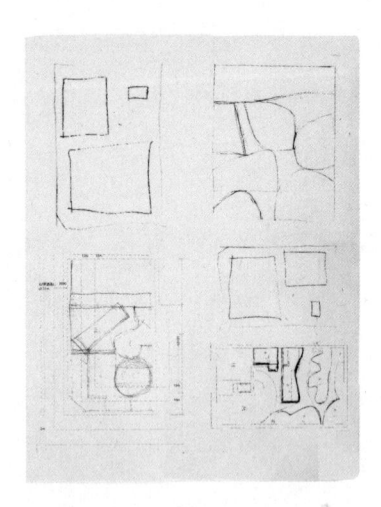

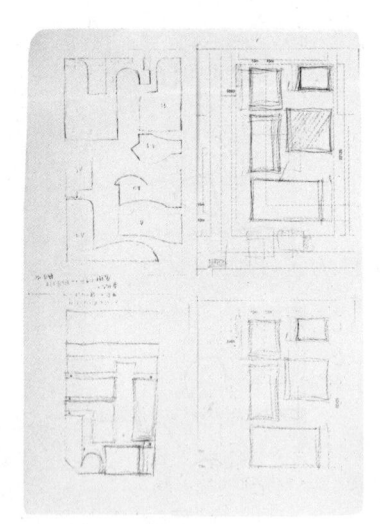

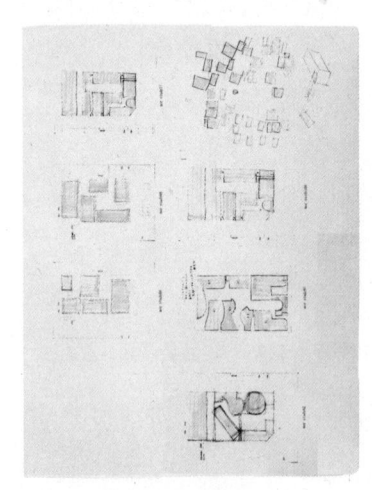

スタディ。敷地にぎゅうぎゅうにつめて並べてみたり、くっつけたり離してみたりする。
Studies for the work: I tried packing the volumes tightly on the lot as well as connecting and separating them.

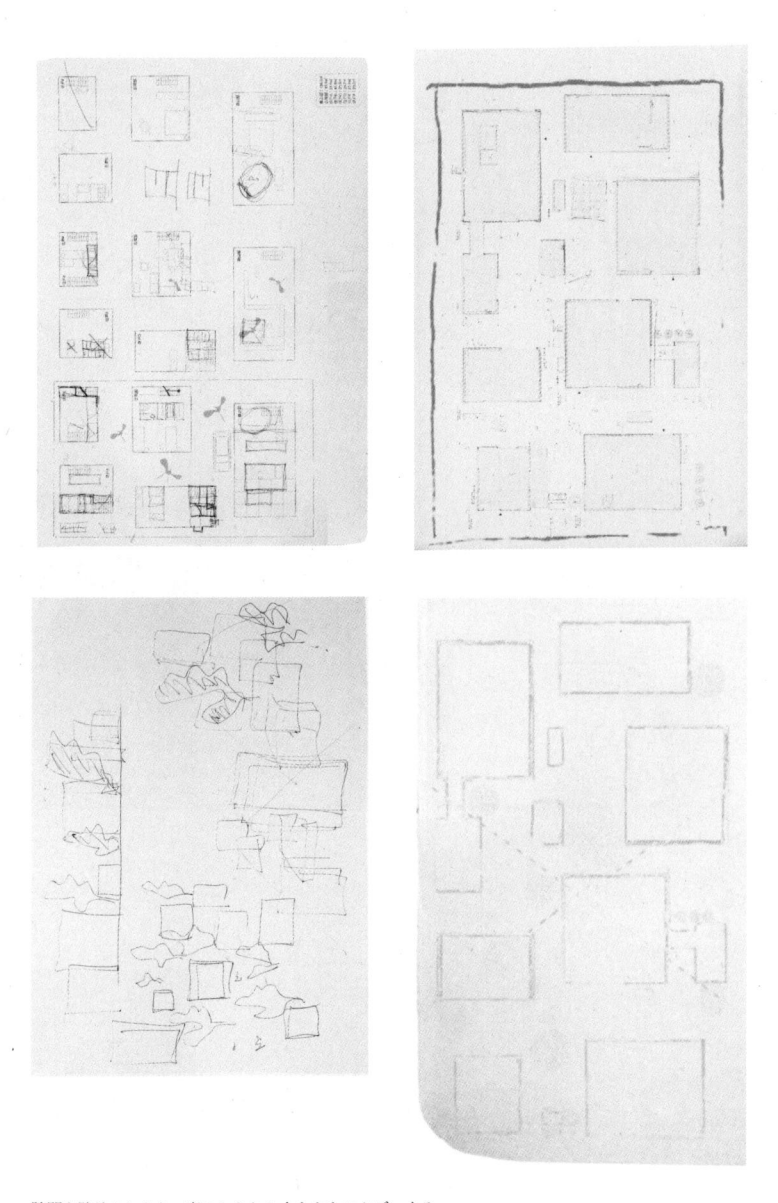

隙間を路地にしたり、庭にしたりと大きさをスタディする。
I studied the size of the lot by making the gaps into an alley or garden.

3. 小さい

小ささについて。建築というものは、人間の身体に比べてたいへん大きい。しかしサイズを小さくしていくと、人体や衣服に近くなり、空間体験も変わってくる。何人もが共有する大きな空間から、1人でしか入れない極小の空間まで、空間と人間の関係が変わっていく。

3. Smallness

Compared to a person's body, architecture tends to be very large. But by making it smaller, it becomes like the human body or clothing, and changes our spatial experience. From spaces that are shared by several people to miniscule spaces in which only one person can enter, the relationship between space and people is different.

犬小屋くらいの小さな家
A small house about the size of a doghouse.

1人しか入れない最小限の空間
A tiny space in which only a single person can enter.

イスとテーブルが置けるくらいの空間
A space big enough for a desk and a chair.

3〜4人ぐらいの大きな空間
A large space for three or four people.

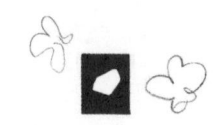

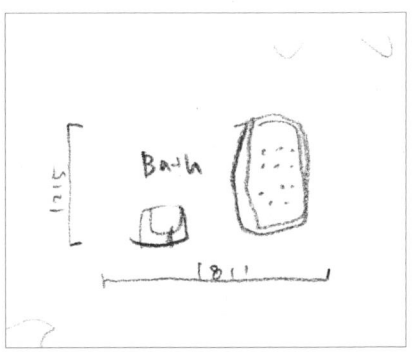

[お風呂］1人の空間。あまりに小さく、庭とセットになってようやく空間になる。もしくは、庭の一部のような、庭に生えているいろいろな植物みたいな存在でもある。
The bath area: This is a one-person space. It is so small that it only really becomes a space as part of a set with the garden. One might also think of it as one part of the garden or one of the many kinds of plants growing there.

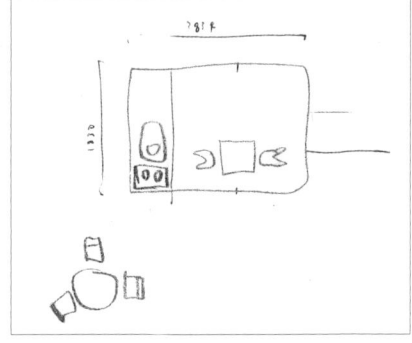

［キッチン］これは2人の空間。2人の人間が食事をする空間としては最小限。この空間は、庭とセットになる、もしくはお隣のおばさんの家の路地とセットになるような配置になっている。
The kitchen: This is a two-person space. It is the most minimal space in which two people could dine. This space could be part of a set with the garden or according to its position might also form a set with the alley of the neighboring woman's house.

4. 環境をつくる

建築をつくることで、環境をつくる。プログラムをバラバラにしていくつもの箱を分散させると、群れとなり、環境とかランドスケープといった概念がなんとなく出てくる。

4. The Creation of an Environment

By creating architecture, you create an environment. By dismantling the programs and dispersing them into several boxes, the structures turn into a cluster and a concept of the environment or landscape begins to emerge.

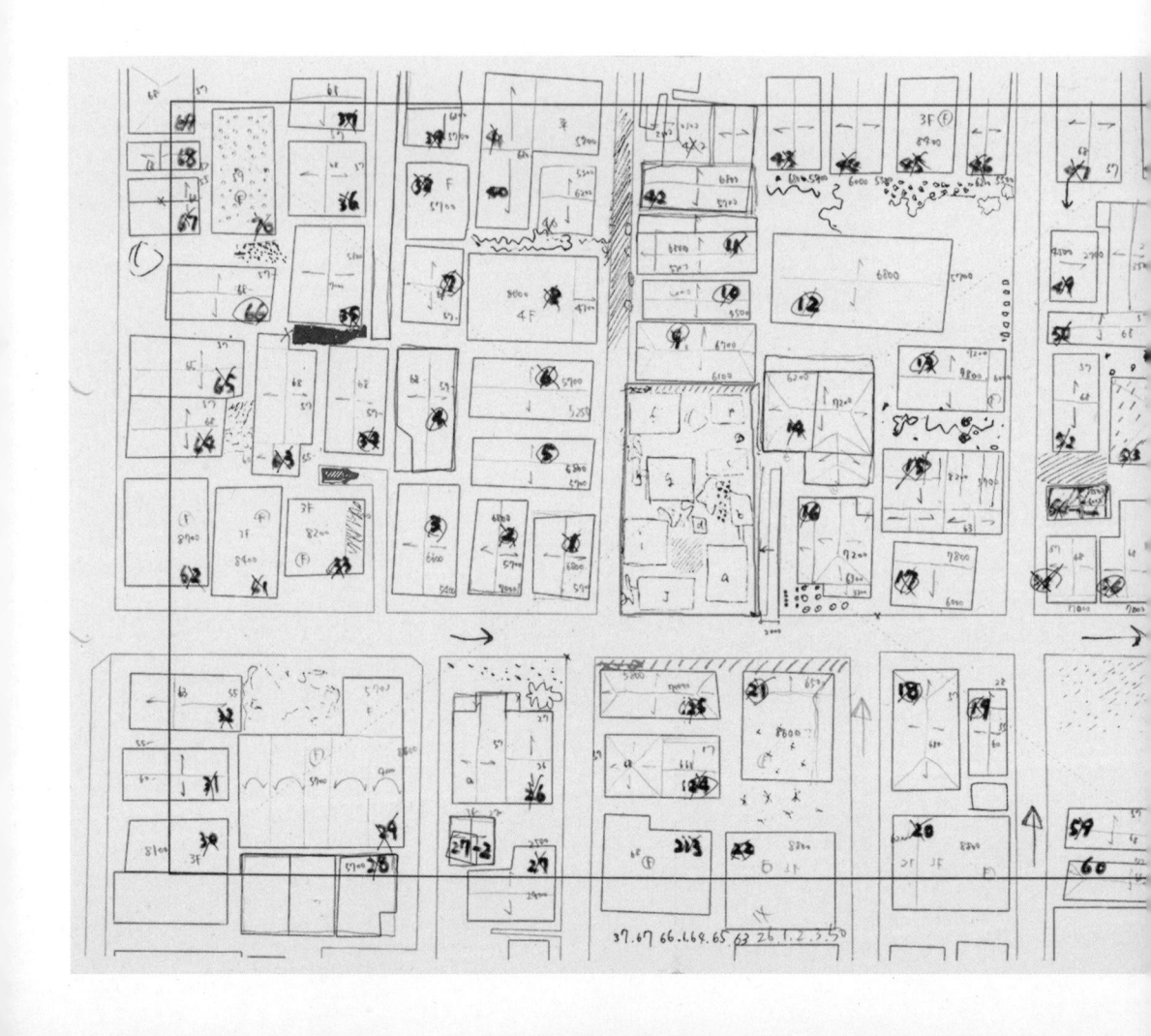

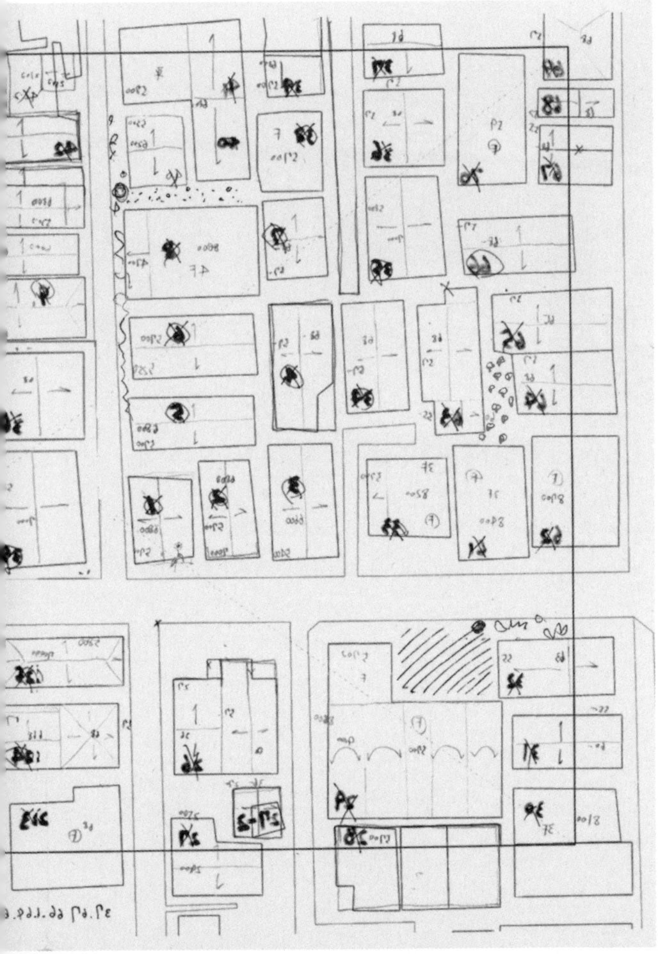

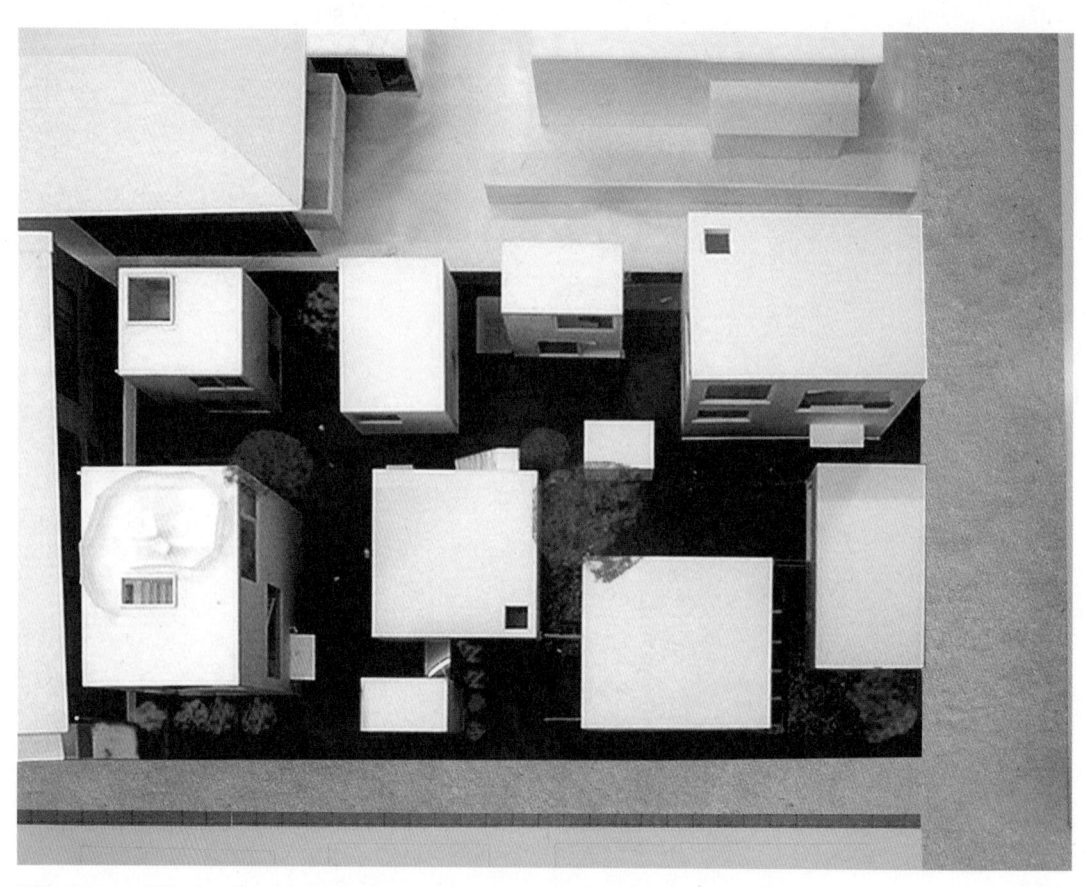

隙間に植えられた植栽によって緩やかにつながっている。
Planting greenery in the gaps leads to a comfortable atmosphere.

森山邸の敷地いっぱい使って結婚式がおこなわれたり、バーベキューパーティーや展覧会が行われることがある。みどりと人、建物と街が柔らかく混じり合う。
Sometimes wedding ceremonies, BBQ parties, and exhibitions which make use of the entire lot are held at *Moriyama House*. The greenery and the people gently mix together with the architecture and the neighborhood.

5. 透明性
5. Transparency

各建築に大きな穴をあける。なかと外が似た明るさになる。
Large holes were made in each of the structures. In this way, the interior and exterior have a similar amount of light.

いくつかの穴はたいへん大きく、路地に直接開かれており、室内空間と路地空間が連続しあう。この建築は住居にも使えるし、お店にも使える。
A few of the holes are especially large and open directly onto the alley, connecting the interior space with the exterior space. This structure could be used as either a house or a shop.

植物と建築が交互に並んでゆく。透明性はいろいろな意味で開放性をつくり出す。ランドスケープと建築が融合しあい、室内の生活と庭の生活がつながりあう。

The plants are arranged in a line and alternated with the structures. Transparency creates various types of openness. The landscape and architecture blend together and the interior lifestyle connects with the garden lifestyle.

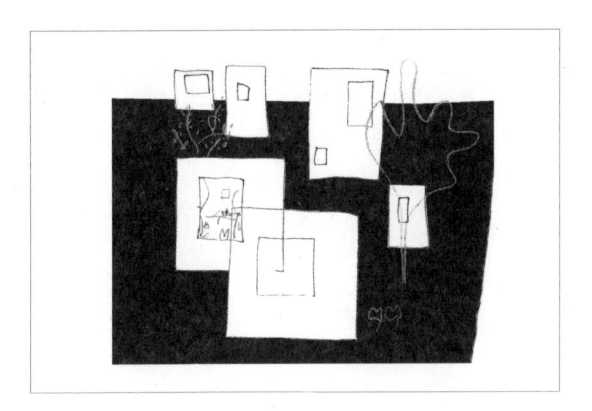

分散配置によって、あちこちに隙間が生まれる。森山邸の向こう側まで見える。

By dispersing the structures, gaps are created in various places. The line of sight extends through to the back of *Moriyama House*.

E棟のキッチンは4面に大きな開口をもつ。
The kitchen in the E Wing has large openings in each of its four sides.

A棟の3階。窓がたくさんあいていて、空にいちばん近い、屋上のようなへや。
The A Wing has three floors. There are many windows and a roof-like room that is closest to the sky.

模型写真
Photograph of an architectural model of the work.

6. 雑居・密集

雑居・密集というのは、同じでないものが密集する状態といえばいいだろうか。雑居・密集というものを、人間が住む場所を魅力的なものにする空間要素として使えないだろうか。

6. Multiple Tenancy / Density

Multiple tenancy/density can be thought of as a situation in which unlike things are crowded together in one place. But couldn't this also be used as a spatial element to make a living space more attractive?

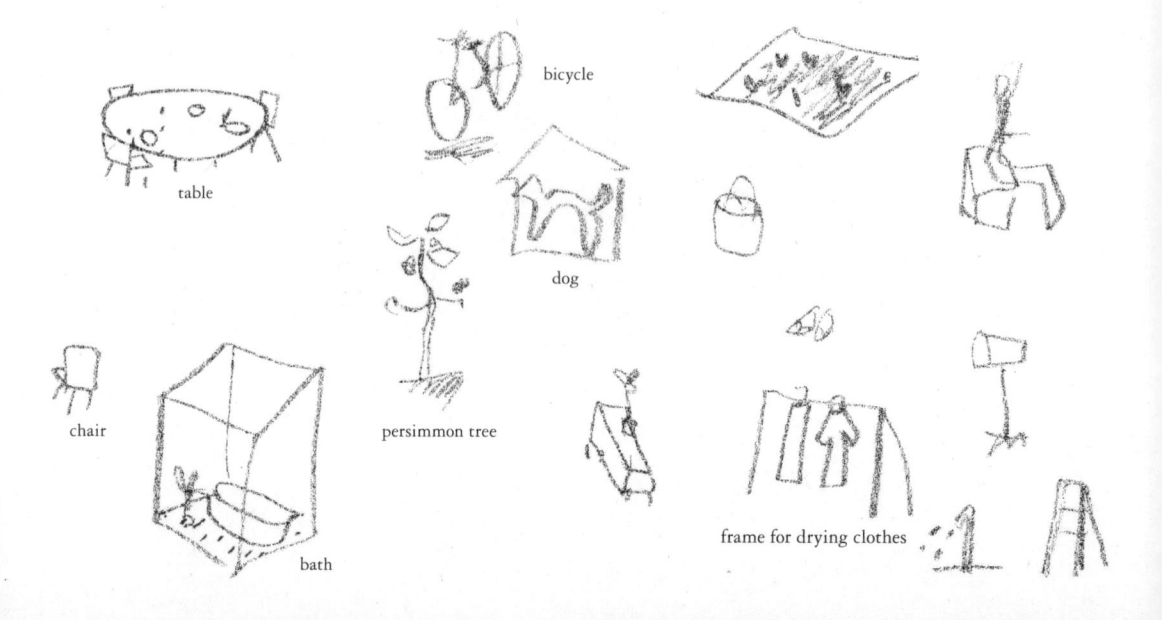

table

bicycle

dog

chair

bath

persimmon tree

frame for drying clothes

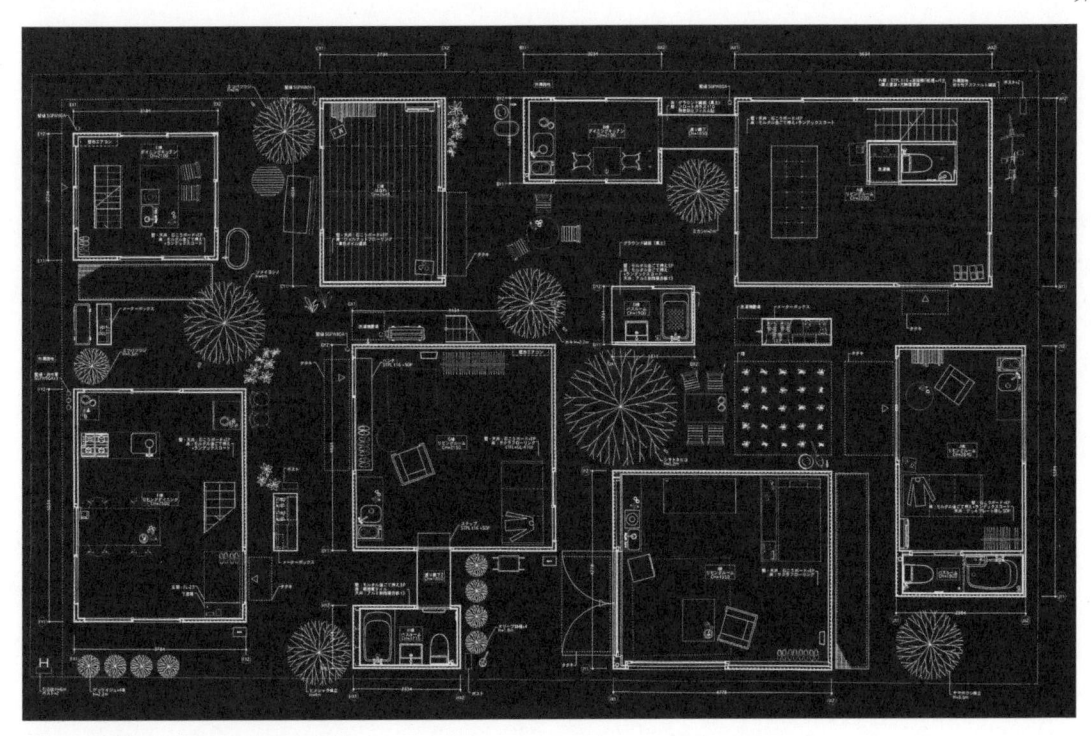

敷地のあちこちにいろいろなものが混ざり合う。
A variety of things are combined on the lot.

goldfish

plant

plantation

7. 境界がない

境界がないという状態がどうやって建築の空間になるだろうか。この街の路地を見ていると、路地で洗濯物を干していたり、ガーデニングをやっていたり、路地は必ずしも通路空間にはなっていない。生活も1敷地内に納まっていない。人間の生活感が敷地外にまで膨らんで広がる、境界がないという状態。

7. The Absence of Borders

How does the absence of borders function as an architectural space? The alleys in this neighborhood don't necessarily serve as passages—some people hang their laundry in them and others fill them with plants. Life can't be contained within a single lot. People's sense of living expands beyond it, effectively erasing all borders.

壁を立てたりラインを引いたりして自分の陣地を表明するのでないやり方で、なんとなくエリアをつくれないだろうか。境界がない、あんまりはっきりしない状態。
Isn't there a way to create area without building a wall, drawing a line, or staking out one's territory? The absence of borders leads to a rather vague set of circumstances.

西沢立衛インタヴュー
聞き手：北山恒

輝かしい東京の最前線

北山 西沢さんと塚本さんは東京の郊外で生まれ育ったそうですね。
西沢 そうですね。川崎に9歳までいて、それ以降は八王子です。
北山 1966年生まれの西沢さんが子供の頃は高度経済成長期で、東京がどんどん拡張していったわけですが、そうした場所にいたという感覚はありましたか？
西沢 僕が住んでいた街は、山を削って谷を埋めて造成した、典型的なニュータウンでした。土地も家もぜんぶ新品で、道路が碁盤の目になっていて、びしっと敷き詰められた新しいアスファルトが、まるで鏡みたいにきれいでした。歩くと足音が響き渡って、「なんて透明なところに来たんだろう」と興奮したのを覚えています。
　通学するときは隣の農村まで歩いていくんですが、あるところでニュータウンが突然終わって、荒涼とした荒野が始まるんです。赤土の大地の上を、コンクリートのトンネルのようなものが空中を横断して、まるでSF映画を見ているようだった。子供達はみんなその下水管の下をくぐって荒野を抜けて登校するんですが、歩いていくと鎮守の森があって、道が暗くて。戦争の防空壕とか朽ち果てた神社とかがまだ残っていて、そこは一番恐い空間でしたね。学校のことはあんまり覚えていませんが、毎日歩いたその道のことはいまだにはっきり覚えています。鏡みたいなニュータウンと荒野と、あと鎮守の森、この3つのギャップはすごかった。
北山 東京が拡張していく、まさに最前線を見てきたんですね。
西沢 そういうことになりますね。
北山 東京という都市を初めて認識したときの記憶とか、都市と出会ったイメージというのは？
西沢 初めて新宿に来たときだったと思うんですよね。小学校の卒業祝いに、親が映画に連れて行ってくれると言うので、僕は一も二もなく「スター・ウォーズ」（1978年日本公開）がいいと言って、新宿の映画館に行ったんです。最初の宇宙船が通り過ぎるシーンがあまりにすごくて、3回連続で見て、「もう1回観る！」と言ったときにはさすがに親に怒られました（笑）。
北山 1970年代後半頃の話ですね。ニュータウンから新宿に来ると、成熟した都市を感じた？
西沢 どちらかというと、新宿はきたないところだと思っていた（笑）。高度経済成長の雰囲気がまだ濃密に残っていたんじゃないでしょうか。
　新宿は地下空間と地上空間の両方があって、面白かったですね。汚く猥雑な雰囲気で、ごちゃごちゃしているその先に、西新宿の超高層ビルが何本も見え、古いものと新しいものが混在する渾然一体とした感じを、新宿に感じていた。ただ当時は子供だったから映画以外は目に入っていないので、都市というものにはまだそこまで関心をもっていなかったと思います。
北山 東京を都市として認識するようになったのは、西沢さんが建築を学び始めた1980年代半ばからですか？
西沢 そうでしょうね。でも、当時の僕としては、東京は都市という認識はなかったと思います。横浜から埼玉まで、なにかだらっと連続しているという感じで。都市というよりはランドスケープみたいな認識をしていました。

民主主義的な東京

北山 現在の西沢さんは世界の様々な都市を訪ねたり、長期間滞在したりしていると思います。そうした都市と比べて、東京という都市は特異だと思いますか。
西沢 そうですね。でも子供の頃は、東京というのは一番普通だと思っていました。なんといっても育ったところですから。
北山 東京という都市の特異性は、どんなところにある

An Interview with Ryue Nishizawa by Koh Kitayama

At the Forefront of Dazzling Tokyo

Kitayama: I understand that both you and Yoshiharu Tsukamoto were born and raised in the suburbs of Tokyo.

Nishizawa: Yes, that's right. I lived in Kawasaki until I was nine and then moved to Hachioji.

Kitayama: Since you were born in 1966, you grew up during Japan's period of rapid economic growth. It was also around this time that Tokyo underwent a rapid expansion. Did you realize that that was the kind of place you were living in?

Nishizawa: The city I lived in was a typical "new town" that was created by leveling mountains and filling in a valley. The land and the houses were all new, and the streets were plotted on a grid and the new asphalt that covered the ground was so beautiful it looked like a mirror. When you walked, your footsteps resounded through the street and I remember thinking excitedly, "Wow, this place is really transparent!"

To go to school, I had to walk to a neighboring farming village, and at a certain point, the new town abruptly ended, and the rugged wilderness began. Across the expanse of red soil, a concrete, tunnel-like object cut through the air—it was like something out of a sci-fi movie. All of the kids went beneath that sewer pipe and crossed through the wild area to get to school. On the way, we'd pass through a grove of trees surrounding the village shrine, and the path would grow dark. There was an air-raid shelter left over from the war and the ruins of a shrine there, but this was the most frightening place. I don't remember very much about school, but I have a very clear memory of walking along that road every day. The gap between those three places, the mirror-like new town, the wilderness, and the grove around the shrine, was stunning.

Kitayama: So you were really there at the forefront of Tokyo as it expanded.

Nishizawa: Yes, I guess you could say that.

Kitayama: Do you have any memories connected to your first recognition of Tokyo as a city or your first visit there?

Nishizawa: I think the first time was a visit I made to Shinjuku. To celebrate my graduation from elementary school, my parents said that they would take me to a movie, and I immediately said I wanted to see *Star Wars* [released in Japan in 1978], so we went to see it at a theatre in Shinjuku. The first scene where the spaceship passes through the sky was so amazing that I stayed and watched the movie three times in a row. But when I finally said, "I'm going to watch it one more time!", my parents, understandably, lost patience with me. [laughs]

Kitayama: That was in the late 70s, but when you came to Shinjuku from the "new town" where you lived, did you have a sense of a full-fledged city?

Nishizawa: Well, more than anything else, Shinjuku struck me as a dirty place. [laughs] Maybe that was because there was still such a strong air of economic growth.

Shinjuku had both above-ground and below-ground spaces, so that was interesting. And beyond that dirty, disordered atmosphere and clutter, I could see several high-rise buildings off in Nishi-Shinjuku, so I had a sense of Shinjuku as a place where the old and the new were combined in one harmonious place. But I was only a kid then and I wasn't paying much attention to anything beyond the movie. I don't think I really had that much interest in the city yet.

Kitayama: Did you ultimately become aware of Tokyo as a city in the mid-80s after you had already begun to study architecture?

Nishizawa: Well, even then I don't think I had much awareness of the city. It just seemed like one continuous stretch from Yokohama to Saitama. More than a city, I think I saw it as a kind of landscape.

と思いますか。

西沢 アメリカやヨーロッパ、もしくは中国の歴史的な都市というのは、マスタープランというものがあると思うんです。ところが東京の場合は、建築を並べていったら道ができた、みたいなつくられ方で、マスタープランはもちろんあるんでしょうけど、相当いい加減だと思うんです。マスタープランが意味をもっていないという、それが風景にそのまま現れていると思います。

北山 東京にはマスタープランが見えない……。

西沢 見えないというか、ない、というか(笑)。ローカルごとには何かマスタープランめいたものはあるんですが、全体として東京はこうあるべきだ、みたいな確固たるものはないと思いますね。

　やっぱり、デモクラティックというのでしょうか。みんなが同時に、いろいろ違うことを考えて、てんでばらばらに好きなものをつくって、誰も統一しようとは思わず、同時多発的にビルができて開発が起きて、そのお祭り騒ぎの結果がそのまま都市の風景になるという、そういう街だと思います。木造2階建ての民家の隣に超高層ビルが突然バンと建っても、誰も不思議がらない。隣で何が起きようがみんな基本的に関心がないような感じがします。みんなが思い思いの建物をもちよったら都市になったみたいな、まさにアーキグラムのインスタントシティが地球の裏側で現実のものになってしまっている、それもインスタントシティがもっていたような理念はない、理念なしにあれが現実化してしまっているというすごさですね。

　あと1つ思うのは、東京には通りに名前がなくて、西洋人から見れば骨格の見えないカオス状態に見えると思うんです。でも、実際に住んでみると意外によく機能しているのも驚きです。郵便物も時間どおり届くし、紛失物はだいたい返ってくるし、電車も時間通りに動くし、ゴミ収集の正確さなんか驚くべきものです。都市計画ということから考えたら0点をつけられるべきダメな街

が、世界のなかで一番安全で、うまく機能していて、便利だという、じゃあ都市計画とは一体何なのか。これはデモクラシーということだけでは説明できない、東京の「普通」とは呼べない1つの局面だと思います。

北山 デモクラシー＝民主主義という言葉を使われましたが、民主主義とか公共という概念が、ヨーロッパと少し違う気がしますね。ヨーロッパのバロック都市のように強大な権力が個人の意思を超えてつくられているのではなくて、個人が全て意思決定に参加できるというような感覚？

西沢 デモクラシーというのは、これはある意味で最悪のシステムなんですよね(笑)。みんなで好き勝手に環境をつくってしまおうということですから。でも、デモクラシーという思想に風景を与えるならば、例えばこの東京の街並みたいなものは一例ではないかと思う。これはこれで、いい点はいっぱいあると思います。デモクラティックな都市というのは、ヒエラルキーや階級性がないことで可能になっていると思うし、都市の風景がそのまま何か群集というか人間の集団に見えるというのでしょうか。生き物の群れのような、非常に有機的な風景で、そこは僕は評価しています。

芸術創造と環境

北山 西沢さんは「建築と都市がシームレスに連続する」といった表現をされていますね。西沢さんの森山邸には、東京のなかで発見された新しい集合形式というものがあると僕は思っているんですが、東京という都市の状況と森山邸には何か関係があると思いますが、いかがですか。

西沢 僕は都市というよりも、建築から考えていたと思うんですね。東京というのは、各建物がバラバラで、お互いに無関心で、そういうところで設計すると、どうしても敷地のなかにしか興味がないような感じになっていってしまうんです。建物も、閉鎖的な箱っぽいものに

Democratic Tokyo

Kitayama: Today you visit a variety of cities around the world and sometimes stay for long periods. Does Tokyo seem unique in comparison to other cities?

Nishizawa: Well, when I was a kid, I thought of Tokyo as being the most average place, but of course, that's because I was raised here.

Kitayama: What is it that makes Tokyo unique?

Nishizawa: I think the historical cities of America, Europe, and China all had master plans. But with Tokyo, as rows of buildings formed, streets came into being. Of course, there was a master plan, but it was pretty slapdash. I think the city's landscape directly conveys the idea that the master plan has no meaning.

Kitayama: You mean, there isn't any visible master plan in Tokyo...

Nishizawa: It isn't visible and there might not even be one. [laughs] There's some kind of master plan in each local area, but I don't think there's any firm idea that Tokyo as a whole should be a certain way.

In a way, you could say it's a democratic place. Everyone is coming up with a variety of different ideas at the same time and creating whatever they want to without any regard for one another. No one thinks about uniformity, buildings are developed simultaneously, and the result of all this festive commotion is right there in the landscape of the city. Nobody sees anything strange about a superhigh-rise building going up next door to a two-story wooden house. Basically, no one is really interested in what goes on next door. The city seems to have been created out of a series of structures that people built in any way they saw fit. It's as if one of Archigram's Instant Cities had sprung up on the other side of the globe. But what makes it really amazing is that Tokyo was realized even though it lacks the philosophical foundation of an Instant City.

Kitayama: You used the word "democracy," but it seems to me that the Japanese concept of democracy and what is "public" is slightly different from that of Europe. Unlike a baroque European city that was created by a powerful authority which overruled individual will, would it be right to say that individual people can participate in each step of the decision-making process in Tokyo?

Nishizawa: In a way, you could say that democracy is the worst kind of system. [laughs] Because it allows you to create an environment in any way that they please. But if you are going to apply a landscape to the notion of democracy, I think you could say the townscape of Tokyo is one example. I think there are also lots of good things to be said about it. A democratic city can be realized because there isn't a hierarchy or class system, and the landscape of the city itself somehow appears to be a community or a group of people. Like a collection of living organisms, it is an extremely organic landscape, and that's something I rate very highly.

Artistic Creation and Environments

Kitayama: In the past, you've said that "architecture and the city are seamless." And I think that your work *Moriyama House* contains a new collective form that you discovered in Tokyo, but do you think there's a connection between the conditions of the city and the house?

Nishizawa: More than the city, I was thinking about it from an architectural point-of-view. If you design something with the idea that Tokyo is a place where every structure is different and they don't have any connection to each other, you end up only being interested in what lies inside the lot. And the architecture becomes a closed, box-like thing. I didn't like that, so at some point I decided to make all of my structures differently. My main motivation was sim-

なっていく。そういうのがいやで、あるとき建物をバラバラにするのを思いついた。それは単に箱を壊したいというか、枠組みみたいなものを壊したい、それが一番の動機だったと思います。

　それと、集合住宅を注文されて集合住宅っぽいものはつくるのはよくない、と思ってしまったこともあった（笑）。要求条件に応えるということだけでは、言われた行き先に言われた通りに走るタクシードライバーみたいで、それは建築創造としてはすごくつまらないことに思えた。与えられた問題を解決するなんていうことは、建築創造の上下とは何も関係ないことだ、と。

北山　手続き的な処理ではなくて、創造的行為としての建築ということですね。

西沢　そうです。対症療法的に建築をつくることに無力感を感じ始めていたんです。

　森山邸を設計している頃、蒲田を歩いていて思ったのは、快適な家をつくるのに一番ストレートな方法は、環境をつくるということです。もし自分が住む町が美しく魅力的で、通りが素晴らしくて、庭が素晴らしかったら、つまり自分をとりまく環境が豊かだったら、住宅が多少ヘンでも、かなり快適に住めると思うんですよ。逆に、環境が最悪で、治安が悪くて、通りが醜く危険で、通りに一歩出るやいなや撃たれるみたいな環境で、住宅だけで快適性をつくり上げなければならないとなると、相当建築は頑張らないといけないし、逆にそういう状態は本当には快適ではないと思ったんです。結局、建築だけの問題ではなくて、魅力的な環境をつくるべきじゃないか、と思うようになった。

　でも、都市から考えるとか社会的な目線から考えるのではなくて、あくまで僕の中心には建築創造ということがあるんです。

北山　僕は森山邸に初めて行ったときに、すごく興奮したんですよ。どこにでもあるような空間の形式なんですが、同時に初めて経験する空間でもあった。それは、「どこにも中心がなくて、建物の外もなかも全部等価」ということ。普通、建築というのはもう少しヒエラルキーがあったり構造性があるものだけれども、それを全く感じなかった。

西沢　中心がないということは、逆に言えば、中心をつくり得るということだと思うんです。「自分が中心」というのでしょうか。森山邸のどこにいても、自分が何か端っこにいるというのではなくて、自分がある大きな環境に包まれていると思える、自分を中心に環境があると感じられるような建物をつくりたかった。「ご近所」とか「界隈」っていう日本語がありますが、あれはつねに自分が中心だと思うのです。たとえ都市計画上自分が一丁目の端っこにいたとしても、「この界隈ではね」ともし言うとすると、その空間的広がりは一丁目二丁目という行政上の境界を越えて広がっている。つねに自分が中心にいる。そういった、制度的線引きに収まらない空間を建築でつくれないかと。それは空間原理として面白いと思ったのです。

北山　そうですね。建築家がつくるものには作為が読めるのですが、でも森山邸にはそういうものが全くない。まるで雲のように捉えどころのなくて、たぶん設計手法が全く違うと思ったんですよ。あらゆる場所に西沢さんが遍在して、同時的にあらゆる場所を設計しているような……。

西沢　スタディの仕方がそういう感じでした。いっぱい模型をつくって、あらゆるところから観察できるように穴をあけて……。

変容する東京の可能性

北山　今回のビエンナーレ日本館は「Tokyo Metabolizing」というテーマですが、東京という都市が変容＝メタボライズしていくことをどう見ますか？

西沢　大きさというのでしょうか。単に新陳代謝してい

ply to destroy the boxes and destroy anything that was like a framework.

Also, I started to think that when I was asked to create a housing complex, it wasn't a good idea to make something that looked like a housing complex. [laughs] I thought that simply trying to respond to the requirements and driving along like a taxi driver to the place that you were told in the way that you were told was extremely boring as a form of architectural creation. Simply solving the problem that you've been presented with seemed to me to have no connection to the fluctuations of architectural creation.

Kitayama: You mean that rather than using a procedural approach, you wanted to approach architecture as a creative act.

Nishizawa: Yes, I began to feel powerless at devising makeshift solutions to architecture.

Around the time I designed *Moriyama House*, as I was walking around Kamata I thought, the most straightforward way to create a comfortable house is to create an environment. If the town you live in is beautiful and attractive, and the streets are and the garden are nice—in other words, if the environment is substantial—even if your house is a little strange, you can live quite comfortably. On the other hand, if the environment is terrible, the area is unsafe, the streets are ugly and dangerous, and the neighborhood is the kind of place where you risk being shot every time you walk outside, and comfort can only be created within the house, you really have to work hard to make a suitable kind of architecture, and even then, you could say that the conditions still aren't really comfortable. In the end, I started to think that it's not merely a question of architecture but that it's also important to create an attractive environment.

But rather than looking at things from an urban or a social perspective, architectural creation ultimately lies at the core of what I do.

Kitayama: The first time I went to *Moriyama House*, I got really excited. Even though it's a space with a form that could be anywhere at all, it's also a space that you've never experienced before. It was as if there wasn't any core, and the outside and the inside of the structure were completely equal. In general, architecture is something that tends to be more hierarchal and has a little more structure, but I didn't sense this at all.

Nishizawa: Not having a core conversely means that you can create a core. You might say, "I am the core." Wherever you are in *Moriyama House*, you're never on the edge of anything but instead feel like you're enveloped in a big environment. I had wanted to create architecture in which you could feel that you were at the center of an environment. In Japanese, we have words like *kinjo* and *kaiwai* [both of which might be translated as "neighborhood"], which suggest that you are at the core of something. For example, even if you were on the edge of the first block of an urban development project, and you said something about "this neighborhood," the spatial expanse would extend past the administrative boundaries of the first and second block—because you are already at the core of the area. I thought I might be able to use architecture to create a space that couldn't be contained within an officially delineated area. This seemed interesting to me as a spatial principle!

Kitayama: I see. At times, it's possible to detect something contrived about an architect's work, but I didn't have this sense at all about *Moriyama House*. It was like a cloud without any firm place to grab hold of, and I figured your method of design must have been completely different. You seemed ubiquitous there, but at the same time, you designed everything...

Nishizawa: That's how my studies are too. I create a model and then make a hole so that I can observe it from every angle...

くだけでなく、あきれるくらい広大な範囲にわたってそれが起きている。今や東京や埼玉や千葉、神奈川と完全につながってしまって、都市というよりは1つのランドスケープと化している。ここまで巨大なものを戦後の勢いだけでつくってしまったことに対して、いい悪いを越えて、まず驚きというものがあります。
　デモクラティックな都市風景というのは、いい点悪い点いろいろあると思うんです。でも、それが何に向かっているのかということは、すごく重要だと思います。今を生きるという現世的活力だけでなくて、何か未来に向かうビジョンみたいなものがあるのかどうか、建築家や都市計画家は考える必要があるような気がします。

北山　パリは1つの大きい権力がつくった都市ですが、その主体が行う未来への投機だったと思うんです。ニューヨークのような輝く資本主義がつくった都市も、資本主義でみんなが幸せになれるという未来への投機だったと思うんですね。同様に、僕は西沢さんの森山邸や塚本さんのハウス&アトリエ・ワンのような小さな建築は、東京という都市を区分所有する180万人に向けた未来への投機だと思います。こういう住まい方が理解され、賛同する人がいれば、インスタントな都市であるからこそ一気に増殖すると思うのです。

西沢　そうかもしれません。そういう期待は僕にももちろんあります。
　ヨーロッパの都市というのは、「変わらない」ということのモデルを出したと思うんですね。壁をめぐらせて、その中を石でつくって、人間の人生よりも長く保たれる都市をつくった。人間の生を引き受けるのだから、都市というのはそうコロコロ毎日姿を変えてはいけないと、彼等は言った。一方、アジアの都市は、「変わる」ということをモデルにした。日本に限らず、香港や台湾、ベトナム、あらゆるアジアがそうだと思いますが、人間の生活は変わるし価値観も変わっていく、人間の生というのは変わっていくのだから、それを支える都市もどんどん変わっていくべきだということを、形で示していると思うんです。それはどちらが良い悪いということではなく、価値観の違いですね。ただ僕は、アジア的都市のそれを単に「今を楽しもう」主義でやるのではなくて、未来への投機として説明できるのかどうかが、我々の問題だと思います。

The Potential for a Changing Tokyo

Kitayama: The theme of the Japan Pavilion at this biennale is "Tokyo Metabolizing." How do you see Tokyo changing or metabolizing as a city?

Nishizawa: First of all, there's the aspect of size. Not only is it metabolizing but it's happening on an amazingly vast scale. At this point, Tokyo, Saitama, Chiba, and Kanagawa are all completely connected, and more than a city, it has become an evolving landscape. Until now, huge things have been created merely with post-war vigor. But things have gone beyond good or bad and hinge primarily on awe.

The landscape of a democratic city has a variety of good and bad points. But the direction it's headed is an extremely important concern. It's not only a question of having sufficient vitality regarding life in the present. There's also a need for architects and urban planners to have a sense of vision regarding the future.

Kitayama: Paris is a city that was created by a single great authority, but at the core there was also a great deal of speculation regarding the future. And then there's a city like New York that was created by "glorious" capitalism based on the speculation that capitalism would make everyone happy in the future. At the same time, I think that small-scale architecture, like your *Moriyama House* and Yoshiharu Tsukamoto's *House & Atelier Bow-Wow*, is a speculation on the future of the 1.8 million individual landowners in the city of Tokyo. Provided there are people who understand and approve of this type of dwelling, I imagine it will quickly proliferate due to the very fact that this is an instant city.

Nishizawa: Perhaps so. Personally, I am naturally very hopeful.

I think that European cities introduced an "unchanging" model. Within walls, they created cities out of stone that could be maintained for longer than a person's life. They believed that if you're going to accommodate people's lives, you can't keep changing the form every day. On the other hand, Asian cities are based on a model of "change." This is true not only of Japan, but also of Hong Kong, Taiwan, Vietnam, and all of Asia. People's lives change, and values do too, and because they change, the idea that the city that supports them should also change rapidly is indicated by its form. It's not a question of one being good and the other bad, it's just a difference in values. But rather than merely seeing the Asian city as something that we should just "enjoy now," I think the problem we face is whether or not we can express it as a speculation on the future.

Tokyo in Practice
Koh Kitayama

洗足の連結住棟
G-Flat

東京は温暖なモンスーン気候帯に属し、年間を通じて戸外生活が心地よい時期が長い。そこでは、内部空間と外部空間が相互に浸透し、公的な空間から最も私的な空間へ視線が通る透明性が高い住居空間が存在する。このような開放系の空間では、プライバシーを計画原理とする近代主義の集合形式ではない住まい方が存在する。

この集合住宅では、密実な竹林の中庭を介して互いの視線が交錯する。この透明な住戸は互いの生活をプレゼンテーションする建具が用意されている。この集合住宅ではこのように生活者が能動的に透明性を選択することができる。この行為によってここに住む人々は収容されるのではなく、この空間に参加することになると考えている。

As Tokyo is located in a temperate, monsoon belt, being outdoors is comfortable for much of the year. As a result, many residential spaces have a high degree of transparency in which the interior and exterior space permeate each other, and the line of sight passes from a public to the most private space. In this type of open space, one finds a way of living that differs from the modernist collective form that valued privacy as a planning principle.

This apartment complex engenders a complex line of sight through a courtyard occupied by a dense bamboo forest. The transparent complex is equipped with fittings that allow residents to present their lives to each other. In essence, they can actively choose transparency. This act allows them to participate in the space rather than merely being contained within it.

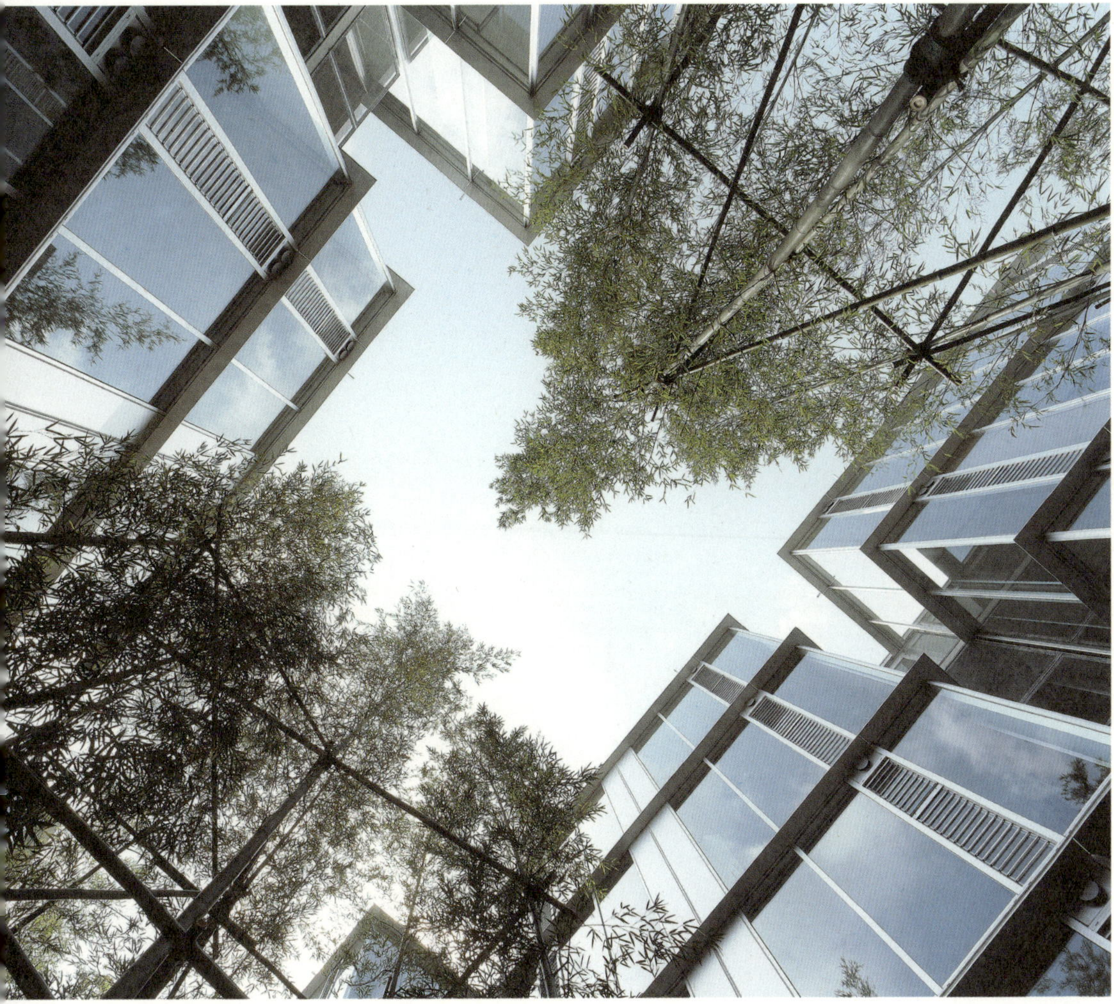

内と外の相互浸透性

敷地の周囲が、木造の戸建て住宅が建ち並んでいたこともあって、周辺の建物のグレインと合わせるように、ヴォリュームを分割し、周辺にも柔らかく、光や風の廻る環境をつくろうと考えた。

Permeability of Internal and External Space

As the lot was encircled by rows of detached wooden houses, I decided to divide the volume, soften the townscape, and try to create an environment through which light and wind would circulate in order to make it fit in with the grains of the surrounding structures.

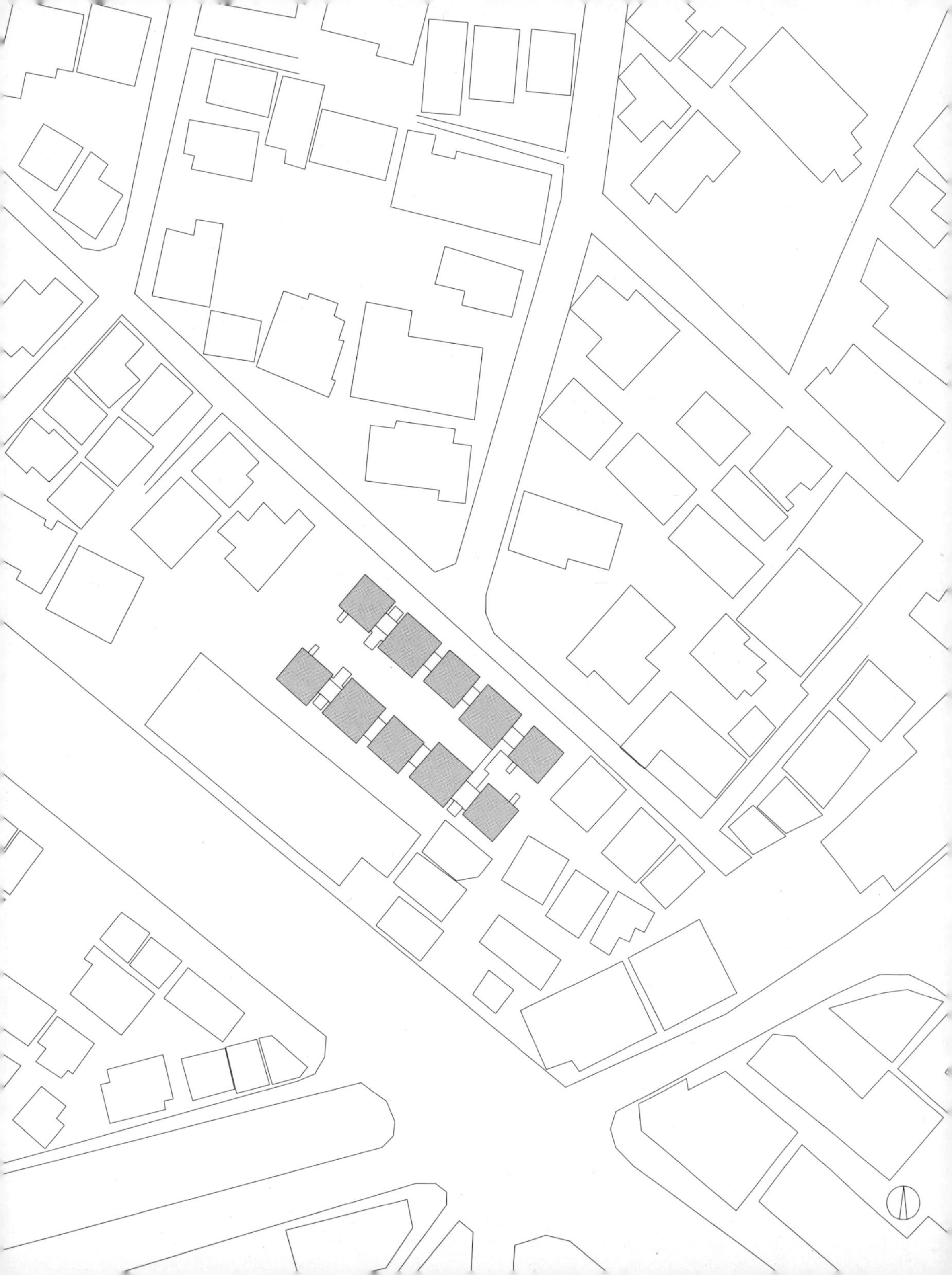

透明性

構成要素を中央に集め、周囲を構造から開放しガラス壁とする空間形式は、密集市街地で計画する場合、建物間の隙間を肯定的に評価し活用する有効な空間形式である。

構造体を中央部にもつことで外周全てを開口部にできる空間形式の住棟を10棟連結したような集合住宅である。外周部は完全に構造から自由となり、どの住戸も戸建て住宅のような外部とのインターフェース面の多い空間形式となっている。

Transparency

With its structural components concentrated in the center and glass walls open to its surroundings, this spatial form is an effective means of affirming and making use of the gaps between the structures in a plan for a crowded urban area.

By placing the structure in the center, the apartment complex consists of ten linked residential wings with a spatial form that allows all of the openings to be placed on the circumference. The outer section is completely free from the structure, imbuing each dwelling with many spatial forms that interface with the outside in the manner of a detached house.

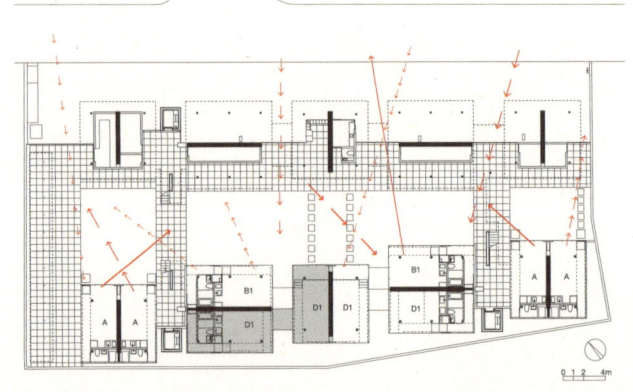

1F

プライバシーを空間構成の原理とする
近代主義の集合住宅とは異なる

これまでの集合住宅の計画では、プライバシーを空間構成の原理とするので、相互の関係を切断する壁の配置が主要なテーマとなる。隣の部屋で何が行われているかわからない、窓からは無限の遠方を見るという形式がとられる。

この建築は外壁が透明であり、視線が交錯するように諸室を配置している。隣戸の気配が感じられることが決定的にこれまでの集合住宅の空間形式とは異なる。

この集合形式はプライバシーを空間構成の原理とする近代主義の集合住宅とは異なるのだ。

Different from Modernist Apartment Complexes with Privacy as a Principle of Spatial Structure

Because in the past designs for apartment complexes made privacy a principle of spatial composition, the positioning of a wall to sever the connection between people was a central theme. This led to a form in which residents were encouraged to gaze out of the windows into the infinite distance, and to remain unaware of what was going on in the next apartment.

In this structure, the outer wall is transparent, and the various rooms are positioned to create a mixed line of sight. The ability to perceive what's going on next door makes this spatial form different from apartment complexes of the past.

This complex is decidedly different from the modernist apartments that made use of the principle of privacy as a spatial composition.

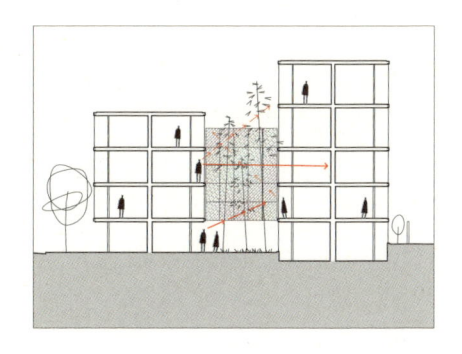

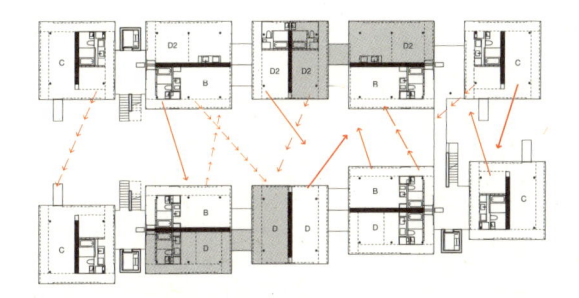

2-4F

外気に浸透する住戸

住戸のバリエーションの多くは住棟をまたいで使用する住戸タイプとしている。住棟間の連結バルコニーを介して離れをもつような構成である。外壁はすべてガラス壁面としているので、自分の部屋を通して眺めるという視点が生まれている。

A Dwelling That Permeates the Outside Air

Many housing variations straddle two wings. This structure incorporates a sense of distance by means of a balcony that links the two parts. As the exterior wall is entirely glass, one is able to gaze freely out of one's room.

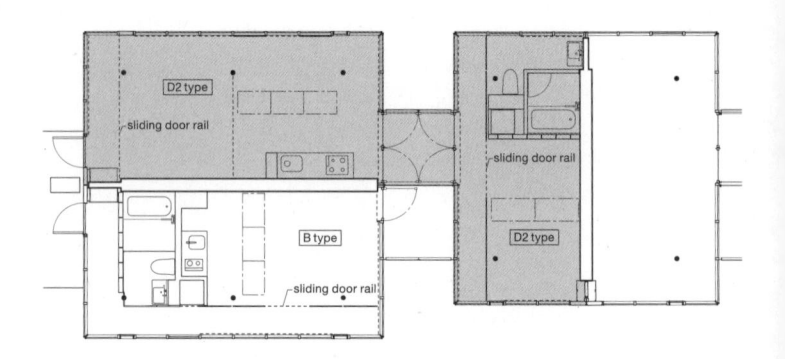

アジアモンスーン地域では、ヨーロッパの住様式とは異なり、互いの生活の気配を感じながら、気遣いをする、という住まい方の文化がある。ここではパーマネントに隔絶する壁ではなく、可動の家具で空間を仕切る、という空間の作法を取り入れる。

Unlike European-style dwellings, in the monsoon region of Asia, there is a culture of being aware and concerned about other people's lives. Here, the walls don't serve to permanently isolate, but rather incorporate the spatial etiquette of partitioning a space with moveable furniture.

視線をコントロールする建具

外周部に縁側のような二重の建具ラインを設けることで内部空間のプライバシーや熱環境をコントロールしている。住戸平面はコンパクトな水回り以外は可動の家具と建具が設けられているだけであり、空間の使い方は住まい手の選択に委ねられている。設計者側からの限定度が低くあいまいな空間形式とすることで、虚実ともに透明度の高い空間が実現している。

Fittings That Control the Line of Sight

By installing two layers of veranda-like fittings on the exterior, the resident can control the privacy of the interior and the thermal environment. Except for a compact area where water is circulated, the dwelling plan is only equipped with moveable furniture and fittings, and the manner in which the space is used is left entirely up to the resident. By creating an ambiguous spatial form with a limited number of restrictions, I was able to realize a space which includes both fact and fiction and a high degree of transparency.

祐天寺の連結住棟
Yutenji Apartments

木造密集市街地から学ぶことで開発される
未来の集合形式

東京では幹線道路に面する敷地は防火帯にするという都市計画の誘導もあって、大資本による大型ビルが建てられている。街区内部の密集市街地は事業効率が低いため大資本の開発は参入しない。この個別解を必要とする街区内部の計画に多くの建築家が参画し急激に建て替えが進行している。

この計画地のある祐天寺は地元の小店舗が元気である。商圏の規模が小さく店の人も住民も互いに何となく顔見知りで気配りができている。このような木造密集市街地では互いの視線が交錯し、互いの生活の気配を感じる。このような共に住んでいるという感覚をもてる環境にいることが豊かな生活なのだと思う。ここには密集市街地から学ぶことで開発される未来の集合形式がある。

Developing Apartments of the Future Based on the Lessons of a Densely Populated Area of Wooden Houses

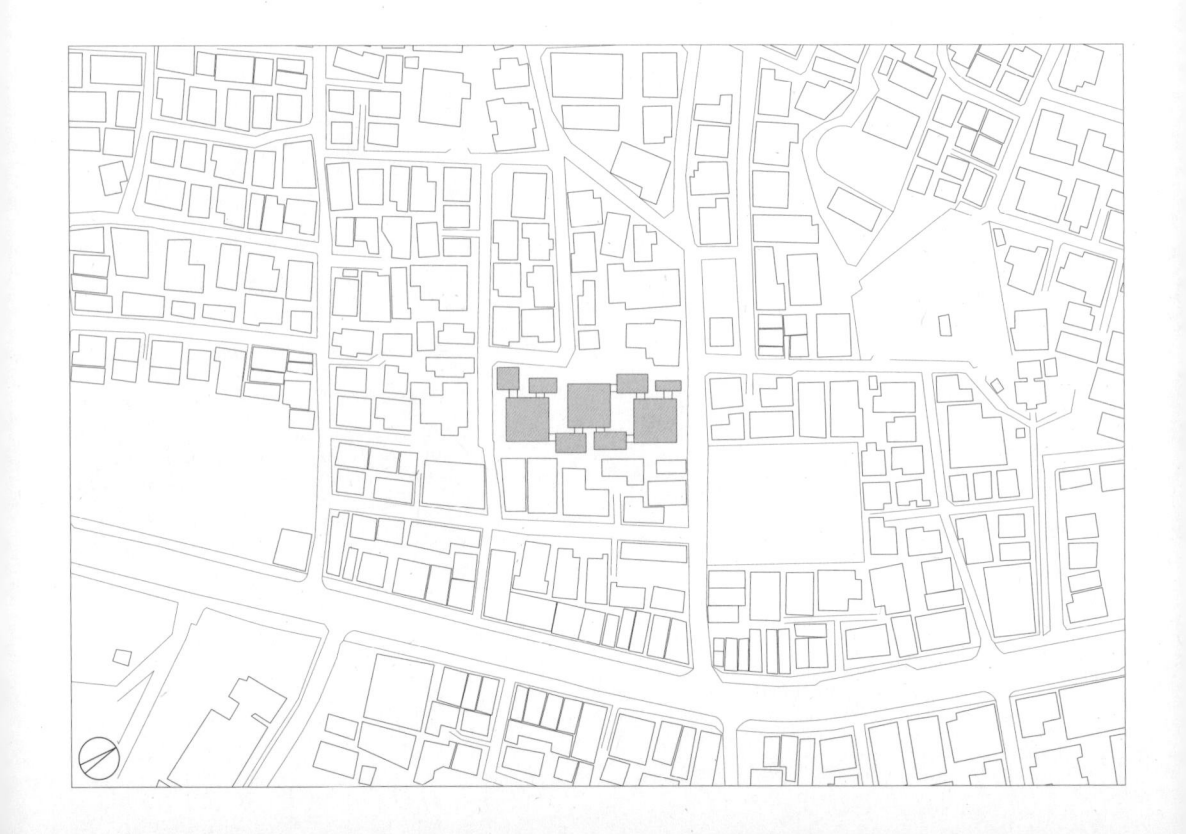

Large-scale buildings erected with huge amounts of capital stand along an arterial road in Tokyo which was part of an urban-planning project to introduce a fire belt to the area. As business efficiency is low in this crowded inner-city neighborhood, there has been little in the way of large-capital development. In the event, many architects became involved in designing a variety of individual structures for the project and rebuilding quickly got underway.

The area targeted in the project, Yutenji, is home to a number of flourishing, small shops. As the commercial sphere is limited, the shop workers and residents are generally familiar with each other's faces. In this densely populated area of wooden houses, people exchange glances and have some idea about each other's lifestyles. This type of environment, imbued with a sense of community, helps create a rich and fulfilling life. Using things that I've learned in this area, I hope to develop the apartment complex of the future.

隙間を連続させる
隙間から思いがけない風が流れてきたり、庭木を通して優しい陽射しが射してくるような心地よい空間がある。

Linking Gaps
An unexpected wind blows through the gaps and in this comfortable space, the gentle sunlight passes through the greenery.

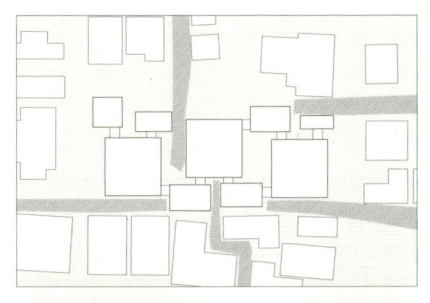

複雑な外部空間

周辺の木造密集市街地は複雑な外部空間が存在する。敷地の中央には透明なヴォリュームを3つ分棟配置、敷地境界には周辺の建物や法的制限に対応するように小さなヴォリュームを分散配置している。敷地内部には周辺と連続する複雑な外部空間が生成される。

Complex Exterior Spaces

Complex exterior spaces can be found throughout this densely packed area of wooden houses. In the center of the lot, the transparent volume is divided between three wings, and in light of the neighboring structures and building regulations, a small volume is distributed around the edges of the lot. Inside the lot, a complex exterior space is created which connects to the surroundings.

121

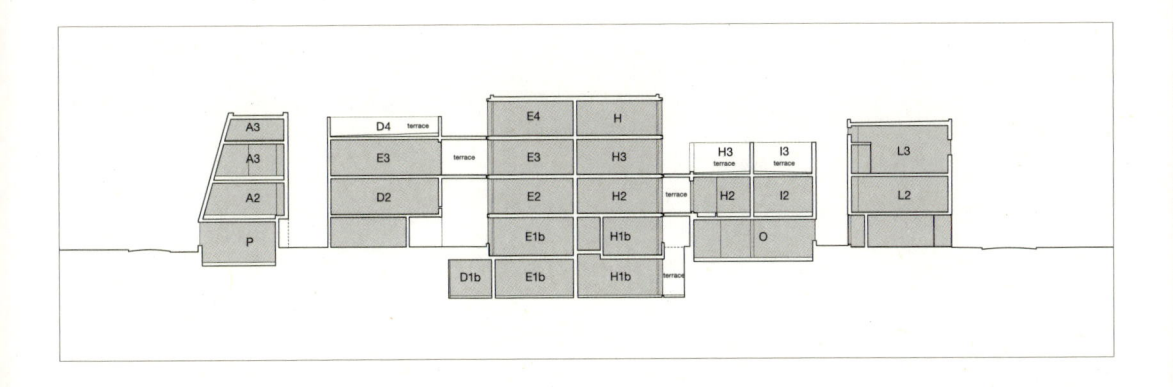

透明性
Transparency

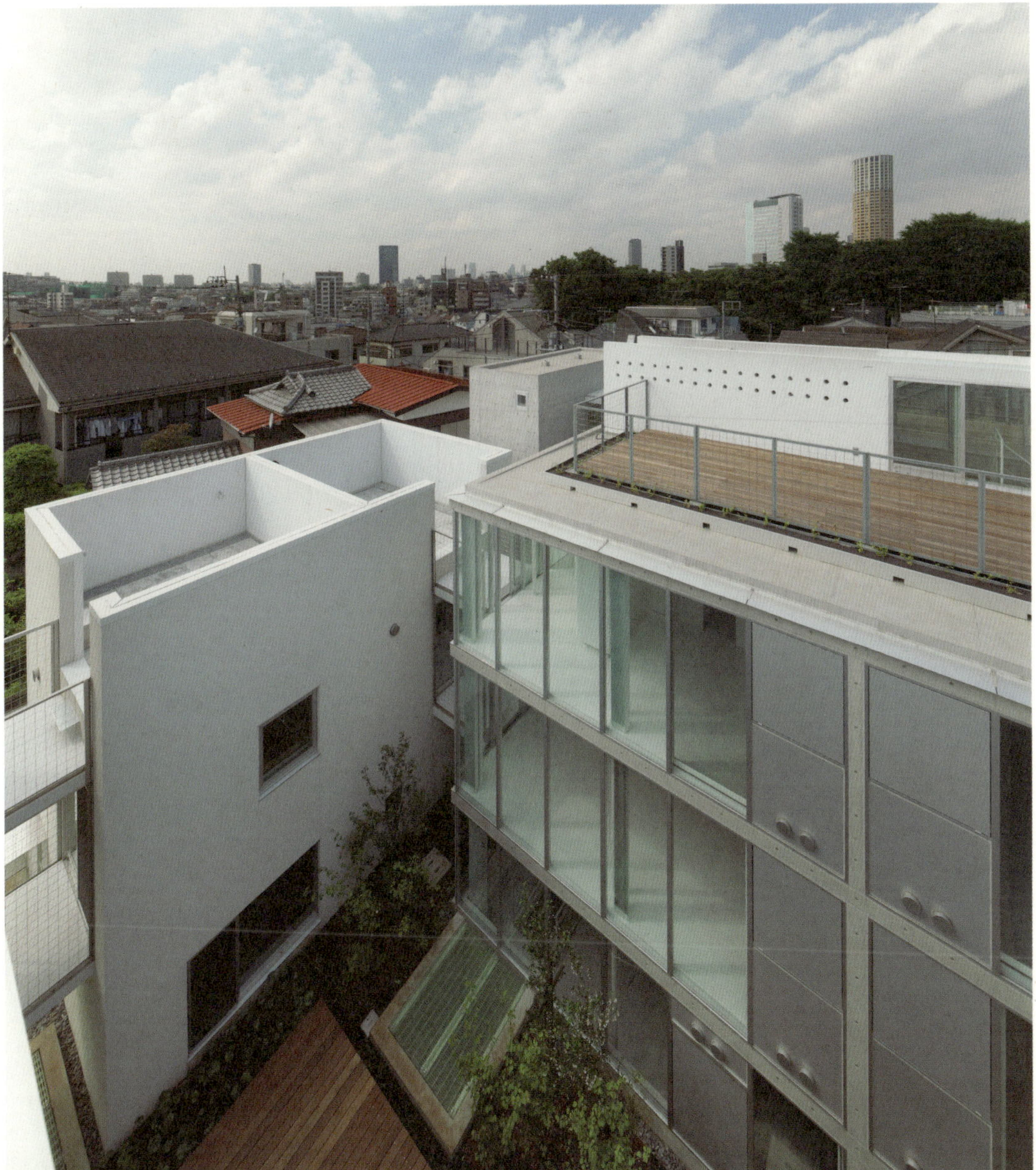

庭木を抱き込んだポーラスな塊

東京の木造密集市街地では、敷地は小さく細分化されているのだが、建蔽率が効いているために空地率は一定である。そこでは庭とは呼べないスキマのように残る空地が存在し、そんな空地にも庭木が植えられている。この1敷地1建物という制度と民法上の壁面後退によって生まれる、都市のなかのスキマや空地を、連続する空間のネットワークであるとして見てみると、この木造密集市街地は密度がそろい庭木を抱き込んだポーラスな塊のように認識される。そのポーラスな塊に身体を入れると、その隙間から思いがけない風が流れてきたり、庭木を通して優しい陽射しが射してくるような心地よい空間がある。

そのまるでカーペットのような均質なグレインの木造密集市街地を肯定し、そのテキスタイルに編みこむように新しい建築を開発する。このネットワークとしての住宅は、それは湿度が高く温暖なモンスーン地帯に対応した心地よい住まいなのだ。

A Porous Cluster Containing Greenery

In a Tokyo neighborhood with a dense concentration of wooden houses, the lots are segmented into small pieces, but due to building-coverage regulations, there is a fixed rate of open space. In these spaces—gaps that are not quite big enough to call gardens—, people have planted greenery. When seen as a network of continuous spaces made up of urban gaps and open spaces that are the product of the "one structure, one lot" regulation and a law requiring exterior walls to be set back from the boundary line of the lot, one realizes that this area of wooden houses is a porous cluster containing an equal density of vegetation. When people are added to the cluster, an unexpected wind blows through the gaps, and gentle sunlight shines through the greenery to create a comfortable space.

Affirming this carpet-like area of wooden houses with their homogeneous grain, new structures are developed like threads woven into a textile. This network of houses functions as a comfortable dwelling space in the humid, temperate monsoon climate of Tokyo.

125

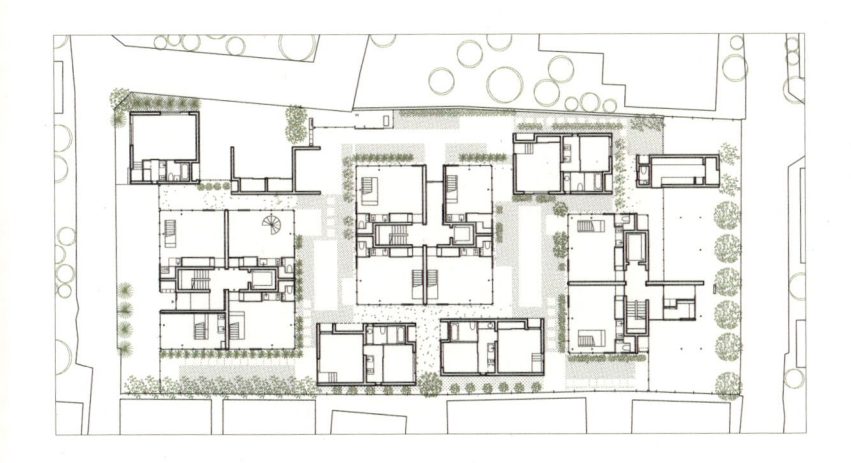

結び

　　歴史上存在したあらゆる都市は、何らかの偏在する大きな権力によって形づくられてきた。近代の都市も同様である。それぞれ成り立ちは異なるが特異な社会的背景のなかで強大な権力によって形づくられる。
　　19世紀半ばのパリでは、ナポレオン3世による帝政の強大な権力の下、セーヌ県知事であったオースマンによって、1つの意思によってコントロールされた壮大な都市空間が1850年代から20年ほどの短い期間に形づくられた。
　　「オースマンの工事の真の目的は、内乱が起こった場合に備えておくことだった。パリの市街においてバリケード建設を永久に不可能なものにしたかった。それにもかかわらず、2月革命の際、バリケードは重要な役割を演じた。エンゲルスは、バリケード戦における戦術の問題に取り組んだ。オースマンは2つの方法をつかって、バリケード戦の防止に努めた。道路の広さはバリケード建設を不可能にするだろうし、新しい道路は兵営と労働者街とを直線で結ぶことになる。同時代の人々は、彼の事業を『戦略的美化』と名づけた」と、パリの貫通道路建設についてヴァルター・ベンヤミンは記述する。そこでは、プロレタリアートの社会的権利に対抗するブルジョワジーの闘争のなかで、都市が政治的手段として形づくられる様が見て取れる。
　　パリはこの貫通道路が設けられることで、都市の中に〈パブリック〉という空間概念が明示されることになった。この〈パブリック〉を明示する空間装置によって、プライベートな空間は切断され、都市は人々を抑圧する装置として機能し始める。パリ・コミューンでは、この〈パブリック〉によって支配される都市空間にバリケードを築いて〈解放区〉と呼ぶ空間を構築する。〈解放区〉のなかで都市の抑圧か

Conclusion

Every city in history was shaped by an uneven distribution of tremendous political authority. This is no less true of modern cities. The overall form might differ from city to city, but its creation through power in each particular set of social circumstances is very much the same.

Under the imperial rule of Napoleon III, Paris was transformed into a grand urban space over the short span of 20 years beginning in 1852 according to the concepts of the Seine prefect Georges-Eugène Haussmann.

Walter Benjamin, explaining the construction of the city's road network, wrote, "The true goal of Haussmann's projects was to secure the city against civil war. He wanted to make the erection of barricades in Paris impossible for all time. With the same end in mind, Louis Philippe had already introduced wooden paving. Nonetheless, barricades played a role in the February Revolution. Engles studies the tactics of barricade fighting. Haussmann seeks to neutralize these tactics on two fronts. Widening the streets is designed to make the erection of barricades impossible, and the new streets are to furnish the shortest route between the barracks and the workers' districts. Contemporaries christen the operation 'strange embellishment.'" As this passage indicates, the formulation of the city can be seen as a political measure to aid the bourgeoisie in their struggle against the social authority of the proletariats.

Creating a network of roads led to the emergence of a "public" as a spatial concept in the city. This approach severed private space from public and made the city function as a device to suppress people. Erecting barricades in urban spaces that were controlled by "public" entities, the Paris Commune created a so-called "free zone." Within this zone, an attempt was made to maintain personal relations without pressure from the city. It was

ら解放される私的人間の関係性を確保しようとするのだ。そして、このバリケードの記憶は20世紀半ばのシチュアシオニストに伝わるものであったのかもしれない。そこでは、パリという圧倒的な都市の抑圧から逃避するために、定住を否定して都市を彷徨い歩くしかないと宣言される。このシチュアシオニストが抵抗の相手とし、諦観として受け入れざるを得なかったものは、〈スペクタクル〉と記述される20世紀に巨大に成長した資本権力である。

　20世紀初頭、ニューヨークでは巨大資本家の台頭により、その資本権力を表象するスカイスクレーパーが建設され、1920年代の10年ほどで一気に摩天楼が建ち並ぶ都市風景がつくられる。レム・コールハースは『錯乱のニューヨーク』で、いくつかのエピソードを示しながらマンハッタンがそれぞれ冠をかぶった摩天楼で埋め尽くされる過程を紹介している。そこでは資本主義が属性としてもつ無限増殖のオートマティズムによって、資本の都合の良いようにヴォリュームが操作される様が描かれる。ニューヨークは街区ごとに巨大建物が構想できるゲーム盤のようなグリッドシステムが存在し、経済の最大効率を求める物質運動が行われる。それはあたかも都市は資本主義というゲーム盤の上でつくられるようである。そしてそこには人間の存在は記述されない。

　21世紀の東京では、イデオロギーが終焉し権力が無力化した空間のなかで、遍在する弱い力（徹底した民主主義）による新しい都市風景が生まれようとしている。世界の巨大都市の1つである東京は、小さな土地に細分され、約180万という所有者に分割されている。それぞれの土地には建築規制がかけられているが、そのルールさえ守れば土地の所有者には自由に建物をつくる権利が与えられている。その

perhaps the memory of these barricades that inspired the Situationists in the mid-20th century. According to them, the only way to escape overwhelming urban pressure was to refuse to take up permanent residency and roam the city. The main target of the Situationists' resistance was the "spectacle," or advanced capitalism, which as it grew stronger in the 20th century created a sense of resignation.

With the rise of powerful capitalists at the beginning of the 20th century, skyscrapers began to be built in New York as a symbol of financial power, and within the decade of the 1920s, the urban landscape was suddenly transformed by rows and rows of these tall buildings. In his book *Delirious New York*, Rem Koolhaas explains in a variety of instructive episodes how Manhattan came to be overrun with skyscrapers. Among these, he shows how volume was manipulated to satisfy the demands of capitalism through the automated response of unlimited proliferation (one of the attributes of capitalism). In each section of New York, a grid system was created to house huge architectural structures and conduct activities intended to produce the greatest economic effect. It was as if the city had become a game board of capitalism—without any regard for the lives of human beings.

By the 21st century, ideology was dead and authority nullified in Tokyo, as a new urban landscape emerged through the ubiquitous presence of low-grade power (total democracy). One of the world's largest metropolises, the city has been subdivided into smaller and smaller plots of land that are divided between approximately 1.8 million owner's. Each plot is subject to a variety of building regulations, but as long as these rules are obeyed, the owners have the right to build any type of structure they desire. Nearly all of these plots serve as houses for daily life, and the structures constantly change through alterations and ex-

小さく細分して所有されている土地のほとんどは生活を営む住宅なので、ライフサイクルに対応して建物は増改築が行われ変化する。だから、東京の建物の寿命は26年しかない。ヨーロッパの都市は人間の生命スパンを超えて存在するため、都市空間は実体として認識され、人には変化は感じられないのであるが、東京では数十年もすると風景を構成する建物はほとんどすべて変化してしまう。数十年の時間を経た東京は、同じ場所であってもそれは幻影のように実体が感じられない都市なのだ。
　東京には〈パブリック〉という概念は存在しないように見える。土地の大部分は、小さく区分所有される私的な生活空間で埋め尽くされている。その住宅地のなかでは、誰でもが交通できる空間と私的な空間が相互に浸透し、最もプライベートな空間のなかに公から視線が通ることが日常的に存在する。この錯綜する視線があるために西欧における〈プライバシー〉という概念は成立しなかったのだが、その代わり気配による人間関係の調停という作法が存在する。この互いの存在を意識する人間の関係性とは、共同体であることが確認された人々の間だけでおこなえるコミュニケーションである。それは、19世紀のパリでバリケードによって獲得した〈解放区〉のなかにも存在していたものかもしれない。
　現代の東京が生命体のように変化し続けるのは、細分化された土地所有によって変化しやすい都市構造をもつからであるが、そのため公私の区分は構造化されていない。加えて、温暖なアジアモンスーン気候に位置することで、外部空間での活動が心地よい。そのため、内外の空間が相互に貫入し、日常生活が公的な空間に浸透している。このような都市状況を自覚的に意識し、そして、それを空間の操作対

tensions based on the owner's life cycle. As a result, the average life span of a house in Tokyo is a mere 26 years. In European cities, urban spaces are thought of as concrete entities that meant to exist far longer than people's lives, and change is something that people aren't readily aware of. But in Tokyo, the structures that form the landscape are likely to be completely different in just a couple dozen years. Even though the place might the same, Tokyo is a city in which entities only exist as phantoms.

The concept of "public" seems to be nonexistent in Tokyo. The majority of the land is filled with narrowly segmented, privately-owned living spaces. In these residential areas, spaces that anyone can pass through blend together with private spaces, and many of the most privates spaces allow a clear line of sight from the outside. Due to this complicated line of sight, the Western concept of "privacy" has never taken hold. Instead, there is a code of behavior in which human relations are mediated through a sense of presence. These relationships, in which people remain aware of each other's existence, is a form of communication that could only be conducted between people in a recognized community. This situation seems similar to the "free zone" that was created using barricades in 19th-century Paris.

The reason contemporary Tokyo continues to evolve like a living organism is that its urban structure lends itself to change on the basis of subdivided land. But because of this, there is nothing that divides things into public and private. In addition, as the city is located in a temperate monsoon climate, it is comfortable to live in external spaces. Thus, inside and outside spaces penetrate each other, and daily life permeates public spaces. A subjective awareness of these urban conditions, and a "new architecture" to manipulate these spaces is currently emerging. This architecture is revitalizing "places that produce a community

象とする〈新しい建築〉が出現しつつある。その建築は20世紀の都市が破壊してきた〈共同体意識を産む場所〉を再生し、人々が主体的に集まって住むという根拠を示す可能性をもつと考える。「東京」という都市はこの〈新しい建築〉によってゆっくりと姿を変え始めている。そこでは、巨視的に見れば多数の個別の意思が参加しながら全体としての最適解を得る見えないシステムが存在しているようにも思える。

　現在中国では中央政府の巨大な権力のもとで、19世紀のパリの大改造を凌駕する都市改造が多数の都市で行われており、そこでは1000万人を超える巨大都市が新たにいくつか出現すると言われている。また巨大な石油資本を背景に、金融資本の活動を目的にして砂漠のなかに忽然と創られた都市が存在する。21世紀は大きな文明の転換期を迎えているように思えるが、その文明は様々な都市群が支えるであろう。東京はその現代都市の選択肢の1つを示している。そして、21世紀の文明に対応する〈新しい建築〉はこれらの都市のあり方によって定義されるのだ。

北山 恒

awareness" which were destroyed by the 20th century city. It also has the potential to indicate places in which people might voluntarily gather to live. Through this "new architecture," the city of "Tokyo" is slowly beginning to change shape. On a macroscopic level, there seems to be an invisible system, which, while incorporating numerous distinct concepts, provides an optimal solution.

In China today, under the huge authority of the central government, urban restructuring projects that far surpass the makeover of Paris in the 19th century are currently underway in countless cities, and several gigantic cities with populations of over 10 million people have emerged as a result. In addition, using huge oil revenues, cities have suddenly been created in the middle of the desert for the purpose of various financial activities. Though the 21st century promises to be a major turning point in human civilization, that civilization will continue to support a variety of cities. Tokyo presents one type of future for the contemporary city. And the "new architecture" that corresponds to 21st-century civilization will be defined by the conditions in this and other cities.

Koh Kitayama

TOKYO METABOLIZING

Data on Works

Profiles

Credits

TOKYO METABOLIZING
第12回ヴェネチア・ビエンナーレ国際建築展 日本館展示

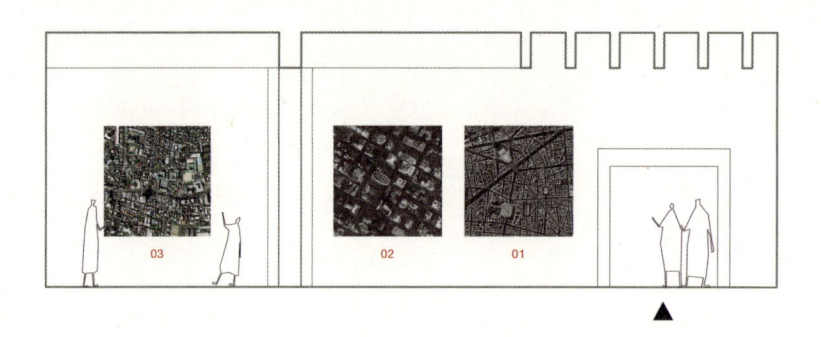

S=1:150

TOKYO METABOLIZING
Japan Pavilion at the 12th International Architecture Exhibition, La Biennale di Venezia

01. City of Monarchism

02. City of Capitalism

03. The Metabolizing City

■ Expanded metal screen

04. Model of "Moriyama House"

05. Model of "House & Atelier Bow-Wow"

06. An Urban Analysis of Tokyo

07. Notes on the Exhibition

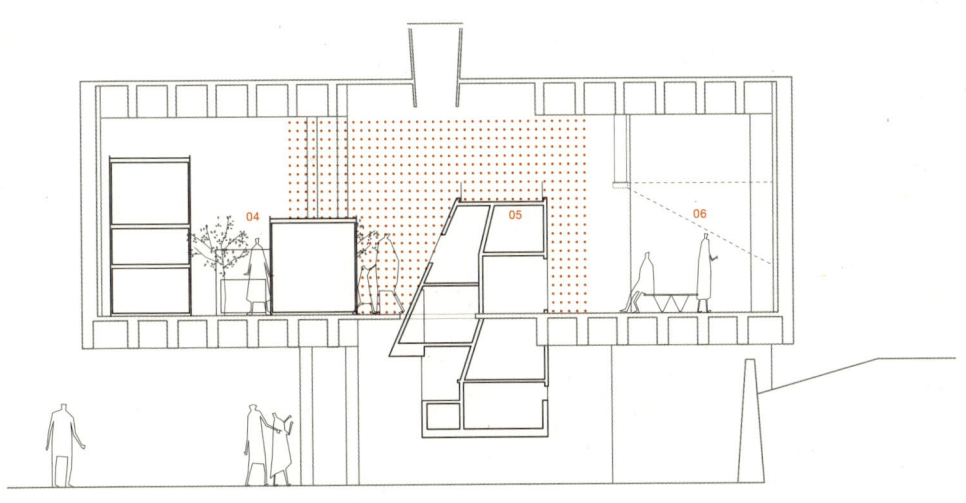

a-a' Section

作品データ

ガエ・ハウス
設計：東京工業大学塚本研究室＋アトリエ・ワン（担当＝塚本由晴、貝島桃代、寺内美紀子、斎藤理、桜井大輔、鈴木悠子、平林政道、富永大毅）
所在地：東京都世田谷区
竣工年：2003
規模：地上2階、地下1階
構造：鉄骨造
敷地面積：74m²
建築面積：36m²
延床面積：88m²

スウェー・ハウス
設計：アトリエ・ワン（担当＝塚本由晴、貝島桃代、倉林貴彦、岩崎淑子）
所在地：東京都世田谷区
竣工年：2008
規模：地上3階
構造：木造
敷地面積：78m²
建築面積：39m²
延床面積：107m²

生島文庫
設計：アトリエ・ワン（担当＝塚本由晴、貝島桃代、玉井洋一、岩崎淑子）
所在地：東京都国分寺市
竣工年：2008
規模：地上2階、地下1階
構造：木造、一部鉄筋コンクリート造
敷地面積：124m²
建築面積：47m²
延床面積：97m²

タワーまちや
設計：アトリエ・ワン（担当＝塚本由晴、貝島桃代、倉林貴彦、田崎慎平、岩崎淑子）
所在地：東京都新宿区
竣工年：2010
規模：地上3階
構造：鉄骨造
敷地面積：23m²
建築面積：19m²
延床面積：58m²

ハウス＆アトリエ・ワン
設計：アトリエ・ワン（担当＝塚本由晴、貝島桃代、高木俊、岩崎淑子）
所在地：東京都新宿区
竣工年：2005
規模：地上3階 地下1階
構造：鉄骨造、一部鉄筋コンクリート造
敷地面積：109m²
建築面積：61m²
延床面積：219m²

森山邸
設計：西沢立衛建築設計事務所（担当＝西沢立衛、高橋一平、大井裕介、岡田公彦）
所在地：東京都
竣工年：2005
規模：地上3階、地下1階
構造：鉄骨造
敷地面積：290m²
建築面積：130m²
延床面積：263m²

洗足の連結住棟
設計：北山恒＋architecture WORKSHOP（担当＝北山恒、挾間裕子、工藤徹、浜真理子、小林由里恵）
所在地：東京都大田区
竣工年：2006
規模：地上5階
構造：鉄筋コンクリート造、一部鉄骨造
敷地面積：1,509m²
建築面積：741m²
延床面積：2,635m²

祐天寺の連結住棟
設計：北山恒＋architecture WORKSHOP（担当＝北山恒、挾間裕子、浜真理子、金栄宇、山下真平）
所在地：東京都目黒区
竣工年：2010
規模：地上4階、地下1階
構造：鉄筋コンクリート造
敷地面積：1,306m²
建築面積：648m²
延床面積：2,751m²

Data on Works

Gae House
Architects: Tokyo Institute of Technology, Yoshiharu Tsukamoto Laboratory + Atelier Bow-Wow
Project team: Yoshiharu Tsukamoto, Momoyo Kaijima, Mikiko Terauchi, Satoshi Saito, Daisuke Sakurai, Yuko Suzuki, Masamichi Hirabayashi, Hiroki Tominaga
Location: Setagaya-ku, Tokyo, Japan
Year of completion: 2003
Number of stories: 2 above ground, 1 below
Structure: Steel frame
Site area: 74m^2
Building area: 36m^2
Total floor area: 88m^2

Sway House
Architects: Atelier Bow-Wow
Project team: Yoshiharu Tsukamoto, Momoyo Kaijima, Takahiko Kurabayashi, Yoshiko Iwasaki
Location: Setagaya-ku, Tokyo, Japan
Year of completion: 2008
Number of stories: 3
Structure: Timber frame
Site area: 78m^2
Building area: 39m^2
Total floor area: 107m^2

Ikushima Library
Architects: Atelier Bow-Wow
Project team: Yoshiharu Tsukamoto, Momoyo Kaijima, Yoichi Tamai, Yoshiko Iwasaki
Location: Kokubunji, Tokyo, Japan
Year of completion: 2008
Number of stories: 2 above ground, 1 below
Structure: Timber frame, partially reinforced concrete
Site area: 124m^2
Building area: 47m^2
Total floor area: 97m^2

Tower Machiya
Architects: Atelier Bow-Wow
Project team: Yoshiharu Tsukamoto, Momoyo Kaijima, Takahiko Kurabayashi, Shinpei Tasaki, Yoshiko Iwasaki
Location: Shinjuku-ku, Tokyo, Japan
Year of completion: 2010
Number of stories: 3
Structure: Steel frame
Site area: 23m^2
Building area: 19m^2
Total floor area: 58m^2

House & Atelier Bow-Wow
Architects: Atelier Bow-Wow
Project team: Yoshiharu Tsukamoto, Momoyo Kaijima, Shun Takagi, Yoshiko Iwasaki
Location: Shinjuku-ku, Tokyo, Japan
Year of completion: 2005
Number of stories: 3 above ground, 1 below
Structure: Steel frame, partially reinforced concrete
Site area: 109m^2
Building area: 61m^2
Total floor area: 219m^2

Moriyama House
Architects: Office of Ryue Nishizawa
Project team: Ryue Nishizawa, Ippei Takahashi, Yusuke Ohi, Kimihiko Okada
Location: Tokyo, Japan
Year of completion: 2005
Number of stories: 3 above ground, 1 below
Structure: Steel frame
Site area: 290m^2
Building area: 130m^2
Total floor area: 263m^2

G-Flat
Architects: Koh Kitayama + architecture WORKSHOP
Project team: Koh Kitayama, Hiroko Hasama, Toru Kudo, Mariko Hama, Yurie Kobayashi
Location: Ota-ku, Tokyo, Japan
Year of completion: 2006
Number of stories: 5
Structure: Reinforced concrete, partially steel frame
Site area: 1,509m^2
Building area: 741m^2
Total floor area: 2,635m^2

Yutenji Apartments
Architects: Koh Kitayama + architecture WORKSHOP
Project team: Koh Kitayama, Hiroko Hasama, Mariko Hama, Kim Young Woo, Shimpei Yamashita
Location: Meguro-ku, Tokyo, Japan
Year of completion: 2010
Number of stories: 4 above ground, 1 below
Structure: Reinforced concrete
Site area: 1,306m^2
Building area: 648m^2
Total floor area: 2,751m^2

略歴

北山恒 
1950　香川県生まれ
1976　横浜国立大学工学部建築学科卒業
1978　ワークショップ設立（共同主宰）
1980　横浜国立大学大学院修士課程修了
1987　横浜国立大学専任講師
1995–2001　横浜国立大学助教授
1995　architecture WORKSHOP 設立主宰
2001–2007　横浜国立大学教授
2007–　横浜国立大学大学院 Y-GSA 教授

塚本由晴 
1965　神奈川県生まれ
1987　東京工業大学工学部建築学科卒業
1987–1988　パリ建築大学ベルビル校（U.P.8）
1992　貝島桃代と共にアトリエ・ワン設立
1994　東京工業大学大学院博士課程修了、博士（工学）
2000–　東京工業大学大学院准教授
2003, 2007　ハーバード大学大学院客員教員
2007, 2008　UCLA 客員准教授

西沢立衛 
1966　東京都生まれ
1988　横浜国立大学工学部建築学科卒業
1990　横浜国立大学大学院修士課程修了
1990　妹島和世建築設計事務所入所
1995　妹島和世と共に SANAA 設立
1997　西沢立衛建築設計事務所設立
2000–2001　ハーバード大学大学院客員教員
2006–　プリンストン大学大学院客員教授
2010–　横浜国立大学大学院 Y-GSA 教授

Profiles

Koh Kitayama

1950	Born in Kagawa, Japan
1976	Graduated from Yokohama National University
1978	Established "WORKSHOP" architectural studio with two other people
1980	Completed a post-graduate course at Yokohama National University
1987	Assistant Professor at Yokohama National University
1995–2001	Associate Professor at Yokohama National University
1995	Established "architecture WORKSHOP"
2001–2007	Professor at Yokohama National University
2007–	Professor at Yokohama National University, Y-GSA (Yokohama Graduate School of Architecture)

Yoshiharu Tsukamoto

1965	Born in Kanagawa, Japan
1987	Graduated from Tokyo Institute of Technology
1987–1988	Guest student at L'ecole d'architecture, Paris-Bellville (U.P.8)
1992	Established Atelier Bow-Wow with Momoyo Kaijima
1994	Completed a doctorate in engineering at Tokyo Institute of Technology
2000–	Associate Professor at Tokyo Institute of Technology
2003, 2007	Visiting faculty at Harvard University Graduate School of Design
2007, 2008	Visiting Associate Professor at UCLA

Ryue Nishizawa

1966	Born in Tokyo, Japan
1988	Graduated from Yokohama National University
1990	Completed a post-graduate course at Yokohama National University
1990	Joined Kazuyo Sejima & Associates
1995	Established SANAA with Sejima
1997	Established the Office of Ryue Nishizawa
2000–2001	Visiting faculty at Harvard University Graduate School of Design
2006–	Visiting professor at Princeton University
2010–	Professor at Yokohama National University, Y-GSA (Yokohama Graduate School of Architecture)

クレジット

写真
architecture WORKSHOP: 18–19, 20下, 25
Elsa Uggla: 35下
Google Earth: 6–7, 9, 24
Takashi Okamoto: 140下
阿野太一: 110–112, 114, 116–117, 119–120, 122–125, 140上
石川徳摩: 37
オカ・マヌエル: 28, 34, 36, 38
釜萢誠司: 22–23
川崎真: 140中
菊竹清訓: 20上
桑原由典: 14, 17
坂口裕康: 48, 50, 52, 56–57, 61
田崎慎平: 54
千田友己: 39–40
塚本由晴: 35上
西沢立衛建築設計事務所: 87, 90–92, 95–96, 98
平賀茂: 68
森中康彰: 60, 62–63

編集協力
挾間裕子
東京工業大学塚本由晴研究室（森中康彰、西村萌、オカ・マヌエル）
アトリエ・ワン

英訳
クリストファー・スティヴンズ

展示
本書は下記の展覧会の公式カタログを兼ねて出版されました。

TOKYO METABOLIZING
第12回
ヴェネチア・ビエンナーレ国際建築展
日本館展示
2010年8月29日–11月21日

コミッショナー：北山恒
参加作家：塚本由晴、西沢立衛

アシスタント・コミッショナー：
佐藤淳子、鈴木真理恵
プロジェクトマネージメント：挾間裕子
会場構成：
architecture WORKSHOP（担当：北山恒、諸橋奈緒）
施工：Harmoge srl
ハウス&アトリエ・ワン模型・映像：
アトリエ・ワン（担当：塚本由晴、平井政俊）＋東京工業大学塚本研究室
森山邸模型・映像：西沢立衛、髙橋一平＋横浜国立大学大学院 Y-GSA
映像（ヴォイド・メタボリズム）：
東京工業大学塚本研究室
映像（The Metabolizing City、解説）：
コーディネーター：田川欣哉(takram design engineering)、制作；wow inc.
グラフィックデザイン：中島デザイン
翻訳：クリストファー・スティヴンズ

ローカル・コーディネーター：武藤春美

主催：JAPAN FOUNDATION 国際交流基金
特別協力：東京都

協賛：
DAIKO 大光電機株式会社
田島ルーフィング株式会社

協力：
CANON INC.
ERCO
WOW

Credits

Photos
architecture WORKSHOP: 18–19, 20 (below), 25
Daici Ano: 110–112, 114, 116–117, 119–120, 122–125, 140 (above)
Elsa Uggla: 35 (below)
Google Earth: 6–7, 9, 24
Hiroyasu Sakaguchi: 48, 50, 52, 56–57, 61
Kiyonori Kikutake: 20 (above)
Makoto Kawasaki: 140 (middle)
Manuel Oka: 28, 34, 36, 38
Office of Ryue Nishizawa: 87, 90–92, 95–96, 98
Seiji Kamayachi: 22–23
Shigeru Hiraga: 68
Shinpei Tazaki: 54
Takashi Okamoto: 140 (below)
Tokuma Ishikawa: 37
Yasuaki Morinaka: 60, 62–63
Yoshinori Kuwahara: 14, 17
Yoshiharu Tsukamoto: 35 (above)
Yuki Chida: 39–40

Editorial Cooperation
Hiroko Hasama
Tokyo Institute of Technology, Yoshiharu Tsukamoto Laboratory (Yasuaki Morinaka, Moe Nishimura, Manuel Oka)
Atelier Bow-Wow

English Translation
Christopher Stephens

Exhibition
This book also serves as the official catalogue for the following exhibition:

TOKYO METABOLIZING
Japan Pavilion at the 12th International Architecture Exhibition, La Biennale di Venezia
August 29 – November 21, 2010

Commissioner: Koh Kitayama
Exhibitors: Yoshiharu Tsukamoto, Ryue Nishizawa

Assistant Commissioners:
Atsuko Sato, Marie Suzuki
Project Management:
Hiroko Hasama
Overall Design:
architecture WORKSHOP (Koh Kitayama, Nao Morohashi)
Construction: Harmoge srl
Model and Video Images of *House & Atelier Bow-Wow*: Atelier Bow-Wow (Yoshiharu Tsukamoto, Masatoshi Hirai)+Tsukamoto Lab./Tokyo Institute of Technology
Model and Video Images of *Moriyama House*: Ryue Nishizawa, Ippei Takahashi + Y-GSA (Yokohama Graduate School of Architecture)
Video Images ("Void Metabolism"): Tsukamoto Lab./ Tokyo Institute of Technology
Video Images ("The Metabolizing City" and Notes on the Exhibition): Coordinated by Kinya Tagawa (takram design engineering); produced by wow inc.
Graphic Design: Nakajima Design

Translation: Christopher Stephens

Local Coordinator: Harumi Muto

Organizer: **JAPAN**FOUNDATION

With Special Assistance from
Tokyo Metropolitan Government

Sponsored by
DAIKO Electric Co.,Ltd.
TAJIMA ROOFING INC.

In Cooperation with
CANON INC.
ERCO
WOW

TOKYO METABOLIZING
トウキョウ・メタボライジング

2010年7月25日　初版第1刷発行
2024年9月30日　初版第5刷発行

著者：北山恒、塚本由晴、西沢立衛
発行者：渡井 朗
アートディレクション：中島英樹
デザイン：古谷哲朗（中島デザイン）
印刷・製本：TOPPANクロレ株式会社
発行所：TOTO出版（TOTO株式会社）
〒107-0062 東京都港区南青山1-24-3 TOTO乃木坂ビル2F
［営業］TEL: 03-3402-7138　FAX: 03-3402-7187
［編集］TEL: 03-3497-1010
URL: https://jp.toto.com/publishing

落丁本・乱丁本はお取り替えいたします。
本書の全部又は一部に対するコピー・スキャン・デジタル化等の無断複製行為は、著作権法上での例外を除き禁じます。本書を代行業者等の第三者に依頼してスキャンやデジタル化することは、たとえ個人や家庭内での利用であっても著作権法上認められておりません。
定価はカバーに表示してあります。

©2010 Koh Kitayama, Yoshiharu Tsukamoto, Ryue Nishizawa

Printed in Japan
ISBN978-4-88706-312-9